THE STILL LIFE

IN PRODUCT PRESENTATION
AND EDITORIAL DESIGN

2   Preface

34   Feature: STILLS & STROKES

What lies between flatland and color county. Multilayered planes and high-flying graphics. Forfeiting depth: Why flatness is the only frank way to strip fashion down to its core. And why Tom Wesselmann's lips cannot lie.

126   Feature: METZ + RACINE

The secret life of the not-so-still still life. The magic in mise-en-scene moments just missed. Products with a feminine personality and why Metz + Racine's pictures proudly show a bit of leg. Generous timing and other luxury goods.

192   Feature: SCHELTENS & ABBENES

Interpreting the inanimate. Probing products and zooming into the quiet zone. Facing fabrics through the magnifying glass. Why the still life is a science of its own. Forget the bigger picture, blessed be the close up!

232   Feature: MAURIZIO DI IORIO

Why a rose is not simply a rose. Beauty beyond romance, soft goods, hard light, and thorny tokens of transience. Vanities and vanitas, Moschino and McDonalds. Cracked eggs, and the violence of vibrant colors. Never mind the message, here's Maurizio.

268   Feature: PETER LANGER

Of style, stories, Plato, and pumps. Reading between the lines of Burberry checks and pinstripe suits. Clothes make the man, theman who set the trend for still lifes to wear layers. Fashion speaks Langer's language, a photographer who feels more graphic than photo.

284   Index

288   Imprint

The still life is a classic back in bloom. In contrast with the immobility of the objects it depicts, the age-old genre has been very mobile, making its way from canvases to silver-coated copper sheets to high definition displays; from gallery walls to glossy magazine pages to infinite Instagram feeds. Still life staples such as dead deer, fruit bowls, flower baskets, and vases can still be seen, but they are now presented alongside the latest pumps, perfumes, headphones, and luxury handbags. These quirky arrangements are of the moment: Fashion magazines feature surreal Dali-like wristwatches next to abstract close-ups of contemporary designer wear. And today's flourishing food industry brings the big Flemish feast back on the table.

"STILL LIFES ARE DESIGNED, AND DESIGN IS A DISCIPLINE, NOT A MATTER OF LUCK."

The still life has always been a fertile field for experimentation—be it back in the days of the Delft School when the genre granted painters the greatest possible degree of compositional control, or in the early days of photography when the medium itself was still very much an experiment. The still life allowed artists to explore their craft in calmness and perfect privacy. While unforgiving technical conditions had once forced the pioneers of photography to work exclusively with daylight, Daguerre and his peers already preferred to pull back into the intimacy of their studios, or oftentimes into the comfort of their homes. William Henry Fox Talbot's first stills feature groups of glassware from his private household and an assortment of his mother's hats.

"Products simply have more patience than people," state Stills & Strokes. The Berlin-based duo, whose pictures regularly appear in leading lifestyle publications like *GQ* and *Interview*, portrays beauty and fashion accessories against the backdrop of paper sets that they arrange on their living room table, treasuring the opportunity to work things out in the intimacy of that space. According to Peter Langer who shoots luxury garments for the likes of the German *ZEITmagazin*'s weekly style column, "some things are just easier without people." Scheltens & Abbenes prefer to compose their stills in the peaceful ambience of their Amsterdam studio, where they can work at their own pace, far away from the industry's hustle and bustle. And according to an obituary in *Vogue*, Irving Penn, who was one of the most prolific still life artists of the twentieth century, always preferred privacy to frantic and overcrowded fashion shoots.[1]

Both *Vogue* and Penn play a vital role in the recent history of the still life. While the latter seamlessly switched between art and commerce, pioneering the creative versatility that has come to characterize contemporary visual culture, the former is representative of a generation of glossy lifestyle publications that granted particularly great leeway to the creatives they commissioned. The realm of fashion may have long relied on models to promote its products, but iconic magazines including *Vogue* and *Harper's Bazaar* were the first to serve as prolific proving grounds for photographers, allowing them to explore ideas freely. Even in the present day, their elaborate editorials continue to provide ample proof that still objects are not less vivid than beautiful bodies. Commercial clients have also long learned to embrace the still life's potential as a tailor-made visual language that allows them to address consumers through artful advertorials.

In the early days of the previous century, when the world seemed to be spinning more slowly and exposure times were still measured in minutes rather than split seconds, photographers spent days in darkrooms mastering their craft. While Daguerre and Fox Talbot had mainly valued the medium as a visual recording method and a time-saving alternative to drawing, Paul Outerbridge, who would later pioneer the three-color carbon transfer printing process and become a prolific commercial photographer, began sketching his compositions on paper before setting them up in the studio. Like most of his friends and fellow photographers, amongst whom were Man Ray and Marcel Duchamp, Outerbridge mainly drew on Dadaism and paralleled the compositions of dreamlike paintings in his early photographs.

"The Surrealist repertoire of fantasies and props was rapidly absorbed into high fashion in the thirties," reported Susan Sontag.[2] In 1943 Irving Penn had landed a surrealistically inspired still on the cover of *Vogue*. It was one of his first commissions for the publication and was strongly influenced by his background as a painter. Both for Penn personally and more broadly for the still life genre, painting remained an important influence, but compositions became more technically crafted and formally fine-tuned, following in the footsteps of Outerbridge, whose design-like approach to photographic composition would fertilize the field of commercial art for decades to come.

"Still lifes are designed, and design is a discipline, not a matter of luck," wrote Gary Perweiler in the early eighties,[3] a time when still life artists liked to portray commercial products with the clarity of scientific illustrations. Shortly after, at the dawn of the twenty-first century, desktop publishing revitalized the discipline, and there were novelties in the medium's technical methods. Digital democracy allows artists to switch between disciplines, to seamlessly integrate photography with illustration and arrive at what Peter Langer calls "photoGraphic" compositions. And since softwares like Photoshop cut the medium loose from its moorings on the shores of the real, still lifes literally became layouts in space—multi-layered and perfectly rendered in postproduction.

The contemporary still life is clearly propelled by the technical possibilities of the present. Extremely short exposure times enable today's photographers to freeze even the most rapid of movements into still moments, filters turn photographs into fresco paintings, and objects have long learned to fly; no matter how heavy, postproduction gives them the wings to hover in space. Spurred by soaring possibilities, the creative industries' blurred boundaries, and the sheer plenitude of our image culture, photographers are teaming up with stylists and set designers. Their compositions concentrate skills to create surreal scenes that combine scenography and sculpture with the art of selling. Poised between playfulness and professionalism, the results are as seductive as window displays, but tightly squeezed into photography's plane dimension to deliver high performance at high definition.

Yet despite the advanced processes and perfectly retouched renditions, technological innovation does not seem to be the priority of the genre's post-digital generation. Instead, many young photographers return to bulky cameras that shoot slowly, countering the breakneck pace of a contemporary image culture dominated by swift snapshots. More often than not, their sets are carefully crafted by hand, some are backed by striking illustrations—and all by compelling ideas.

As Paul Outerbridge once wrote in his book titled *Photographing in Color*, "to put life into inanimate objects requires imagination,"[4] and imagination is a gift that this generation of still life artists proves to possess in abundance. The field of fashion in particular continues to allow artists to experiment, test new styles, reinterpret traditions, and let their ideas have free reign. Flipping through today's lifestyle magazines you find the latest luxury must-haves mingled with historical references, ranging from painterly realism to pop and pulp fiction.

The richly set tables captured by Oliver Schwarzwald and styled by Christoph Himmel clearly follow in the footsteps of the Old Masters. Maurizio Di Iorio reinvents still life staples such as vanitas and memento mori with post-digital punch. Happily hopping back in time, many contemporary creatives resort to the repertoire of the New Objectivity and related modernist art movements. Surrealism, Dada, and Cubism remain important influences, and much like Dali, Duchamp, and Delaunay, contemporary photographers Charles Negre, Qiu Yang, and Philippe Fragniere incorporate chance, unexpected juxtapositions, and literary allusions into their images. Sometimes, their symbolically laden compositions point to haute couture's inaccessibility, but as Roland Barthes rightly remarked with regard to "ornamental" food still lifes featured in *Elle* magazine in the fifties, "consumption can perfectly well be accomplished simply by looking."

Brimful with richly set table tops, fashion flats, collages in space, installations, and photographic illustrations, this book showcases new directions in product portraiture by some of our time's most imaginative photographers, art directors, designers, and stylists. Imbued with unexpected liveliness, their stills unleash the inanimate object's innate urge to communicate. Some examples speak subtly, others scream, but none are entirely still, short of stories, expressive power, or pictorial momentum. Occasionally, they even belie the still life's motionless nature with razor-sharp freeze frames of spilling liquids, bringing old Muybridge back to mind.

Bridging between past and present, art and commerce, dead game and lifestyle gadgets, the genre of the photographic still life lures us toward new but also old trails. And no matter whether their compositions are too tidy to be true or as cram-packed as our present: Much like eighteenth century Dutch paintings, today's still lifes are displays of abundance. Perhaps they celebrate consumption. But most importantly, imagination.

1 REMEMBERING IRVING PENN – THE STRANGER BEHIND THE CAMERA, by Jay Fielden, Vogue, Nov. Issue 2004

2 Susan Sontag, ON PHOTOGRAPHY, Allan Lane, London, 1978

3 Gery Perweiler, SECRETS OF STUDIO STILL LIFE PHOTOGRAPHY, Amphoto Books, New York, 1984

4 Paul Outerbridge, PHOTOGRAPHING IN COLOR, Random House, New York, 1940

Editorial Project for FLAIR MAGAZINE

Photography JENNY VAN SOMMERS Set Design RACHEL THOMAS

Editorial Project for L'OFFICIEL ITALIA   Photography | Styling   LISELOTTE WATKINS

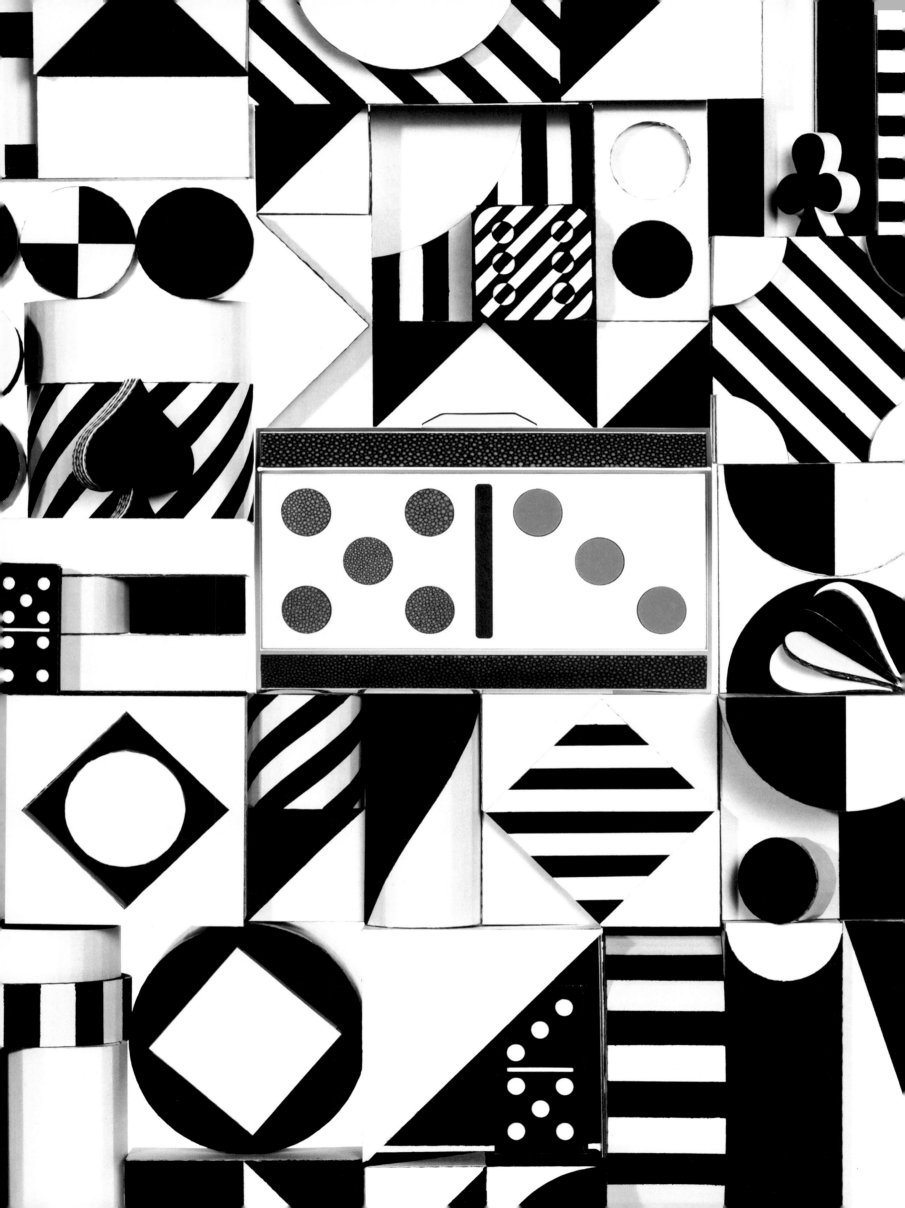

Editorial Project for ANYA   Photography   JENNY VAN SOMMERS   Set Design   RACHEL THOMAS

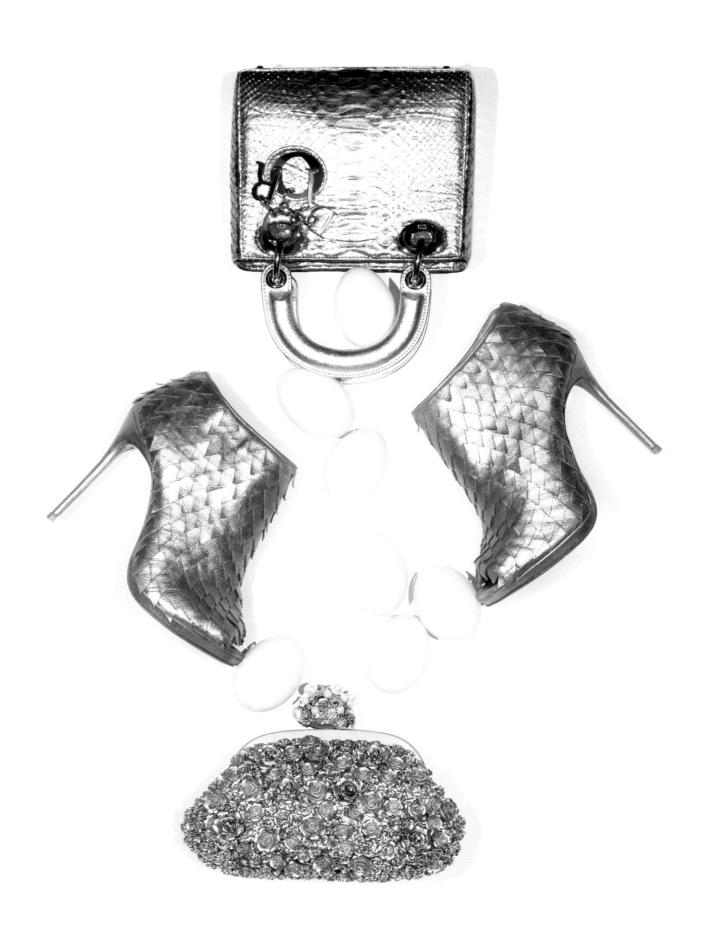

Editorial Project for ELLE ITALY

Photography | Art Direction | MARCELO KRASILCIC | Styling | BENEDETTA DELL'ORTO

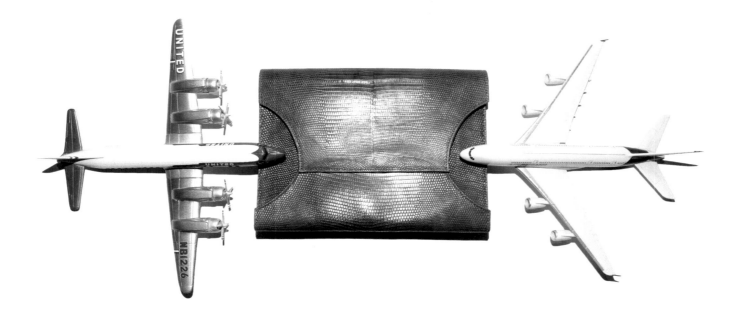

Editorial Project for 1Ø　　　　Photography　|　Art Direction　|　Styling　　　MARCELO KRASILCIC

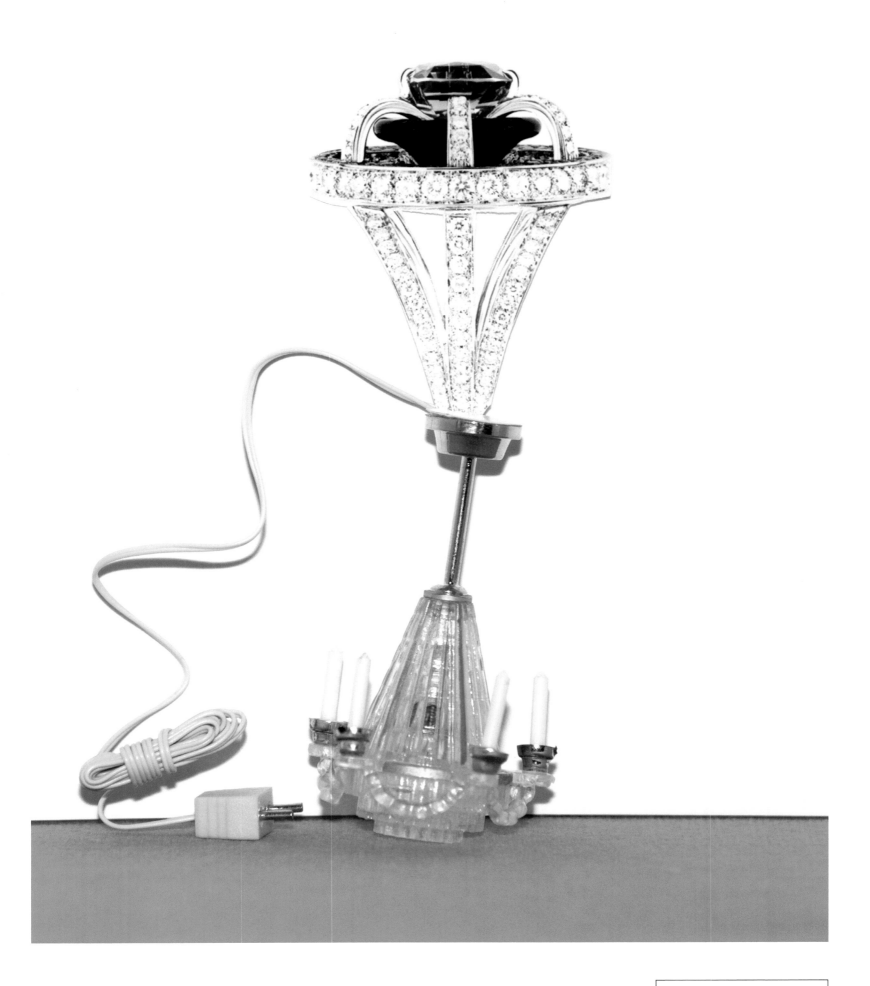

Photography　　JESS BONHAM　　Art Direction　　JESS BONHAM | ANNA LOMAX　　Styling　　ANNA LOMAX

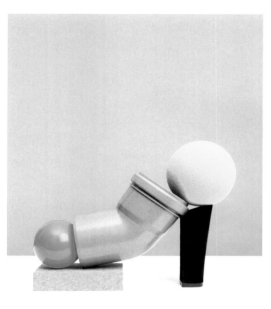

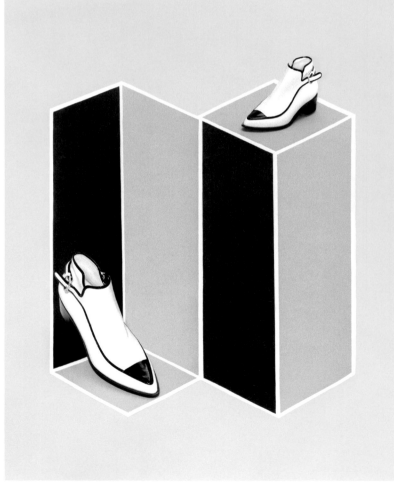

Editorial Project for ELLE UK   Photography   QIU YANG   Set Design   QIU YANG | MICHAEL SCHONER

Advertorial Project for WALLPAPER*   Photography QIU YANG   Set Design ELENA MORA

Editorial Project for T MAGAZINE CHINA

Photography | QIU YANG | Set Design | QIU YANG | SARAH-JANE HOFFMANN | Styling | SARAH-JANE HOFFMANN

Editorial Project for SÜDDEUTSCHE ZEITUNG MAGAZIN

Photography   QIU YANG   Set Design   QIU YANG | SARAH-JANE HOFFMANN

In the lush world of Stills & Strokes, photography, illustration, and paper craft collide. High heels and low shoes fall in love in the light of paper-made moons, and printouts escape their planar existence to protrude into space. The laws of physics are pleasantly loose in this world. And lips are as luscious as the ones in Tom Wesselmann's paintings.

Editorial Project for SLEEK

Photography | Styling | Set Design | STILLS & STROKES | Concept | FINJA ROSENTHAL |

Stills & Strokes stands for still lifes and brush stokes. Less literally, it also stands for Stefan Vorbeck, a graphic designer turned photographer, and Melanie Homann, a former art director and editorial designer. Her vivid patterns set the tone for Stills & Strokes's colorful compositions. Digitally drawn and then printed on paper to be built into sets, they counter sober studio curves with great graphic punch. And instead of merely providing the setting for a product, Homann's illustrations engage it in dialogue—a dialogue of different dimensions. ▷

Corporate Publishing Project for KADEWE

Photography | Styling | Set Design | STILLS & STROKES | Art Direction | MARIO LOMBARDO

Stills & Strokes's still lifes live on the interplay of picture planes, but they also promote their integration: while other photographers try hard to make the product and its most delicate details stand out, the Berlin-based duo works the product so it melts with the bold backdrops.

"The picture is finished once its object doesn't feel foreign to the illustration anymore, and that is usually when things forfeit their depth, as details begin to dissolve," the duo declares. Indeed, Vorbeck's precise lighting lets details dissolve for the benefit of bold, pithy pictures. It does not emphasize precious materials, extras, or elaborate features, but swallows them, pushing the product out of its physical dimension into the flatness of the picture, almost as if to ask: Aren't details overrated, anyway? And high definition along with photorealism, too?

"We prefer our pictures to look less photographic. If there was the time, I would eventually just paint everything," Homann jokes. Looking at her patterns, Homann's paintings would probably be all graphic and abstract. Perhaps reminiscent of those Clement Greenberg referred to when arguing that flatness was the only frank way for art to strip things down to their truthful core. In modernist painting, the flat representation of objects was meant to overcome old ideals and recognize that the image's reality is that of a flat object. In the case of Stills & Strokes's photographs, it means a playful denial of depth: the reality of the fashion product is not profound but bold and simple, Stills & Strokes say.

There is not much room for philosophy in commercial photography, and compared to the minimalist idea that art can exist in and of itself, commercial still life photography cannot—it needs its products and caters to clients. In Stills & Strokes' case, most commissions come from the editorial field, which usually allows for a fair amount of creative leeway. Periodically working with *GQ* Italy and the German edition of Andy Warhol's *Interview* magazine, the duo has found platforms that foster creativity and certainly welcome a dash of pop. Pop culture references spill out of Stills & Strokes photos, some compositions clearly citing Pop Art, one of the movements that Greenberg's plea for flatness had paved the way for. While Wesselmann, Warhol, and Co. liked to take their still lifes to the level of gigantism, Stills & Strokes's tend to be of small scale, usually little enough to be put together on their living room table.

Stills & Strokes started as a side-project when Homann ▷

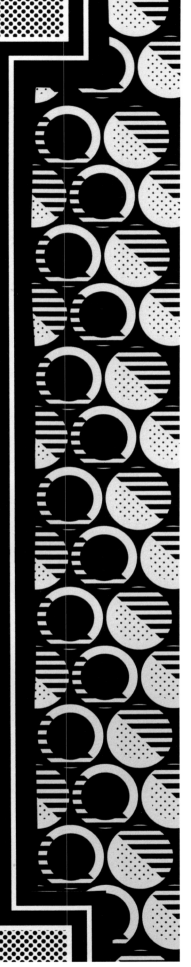

Editorial Project for INTERVIEW GERMANY   Photography | Styling | Set Design   STILLS & STROKES

Photography | Set Design | Styling | STILLS & STROKES

Editorial Project for GARAGE   Photography | Styling | Set Design   STILLS & STROKES

still worked full time as an art director at the Cologne office of design consultancy Meiré und Meiré, and Vorbeck freelanced, mainly as an assistant in fashion photography. Both communication designers by education, the two met during their studies, became a couple, and collaborated since the early days of their careers when commissions allowed for it. "Still lifes have always been something we liked to do as a team, a mode of collaboration that connected us throughout our diverging paths, but we never really planned to specialize in it," both of them share. They simply started step by step with smaller commissions, until requests for still lifes started to come in more regularly approximately two years ago. Homann had showed their still life portfolio to her ex-employer, Mike Meiré, before she left the studio, and he had encouraged her to pursue the project and collaborate. Amongst the first jobs they realized jointly was a feature for *Interview* magazine, one of Meiré and Meiré's editorial clients. The one-off commission would turn into an ongoing series of photographs for every *Interview* issue, and Homann and Vorbeck would set up Stills & Strokes in Berlin.

Their stills are collages in space, breaking the barriers between creative disciplines and spatial dimensions. Graphic designers at heart, Homann and Vorbeck compare their image-making process to gradually developing layouts in InDesign. But while they describe their way of working as "a matter of putting things together, pushing them back and forth until one arrives at a final composition," their creations clearly suggest that they gladly work beyond grids— and beyond the digital sphere of Adobe's Creative Suite.

"Looking at the products we portray, paper sets feel most appropriate since they are light and more honest than profound stagings with plenty of props," Homann says. "Also, some things have to be built to be comprehended," Vorbeck adds, regarding their analogue sets. "Sure, it would be possible to break all this down to layers and build the image digitally—but then you wouldn't feel each element as a building block of the composition. It's a very different approach, although in the end one may hardly be able to tell the difference."

Model making is based on illusion and more often than not, model makers' illusions strive to simulate the real. In Stills & Strokes pictures, reality does not seem to play a significant role. They do not aim to persuade, but play with techniques, dimensions, and human perception. And sometimes, perception plays tricks on them: "There have been cases where the physical features were lost in reproduction," says Vorbeck. "Or vice versa, it has happened that a pattern looked physical enough to evoke multiple layers where there was in fact only one flat print- ▷

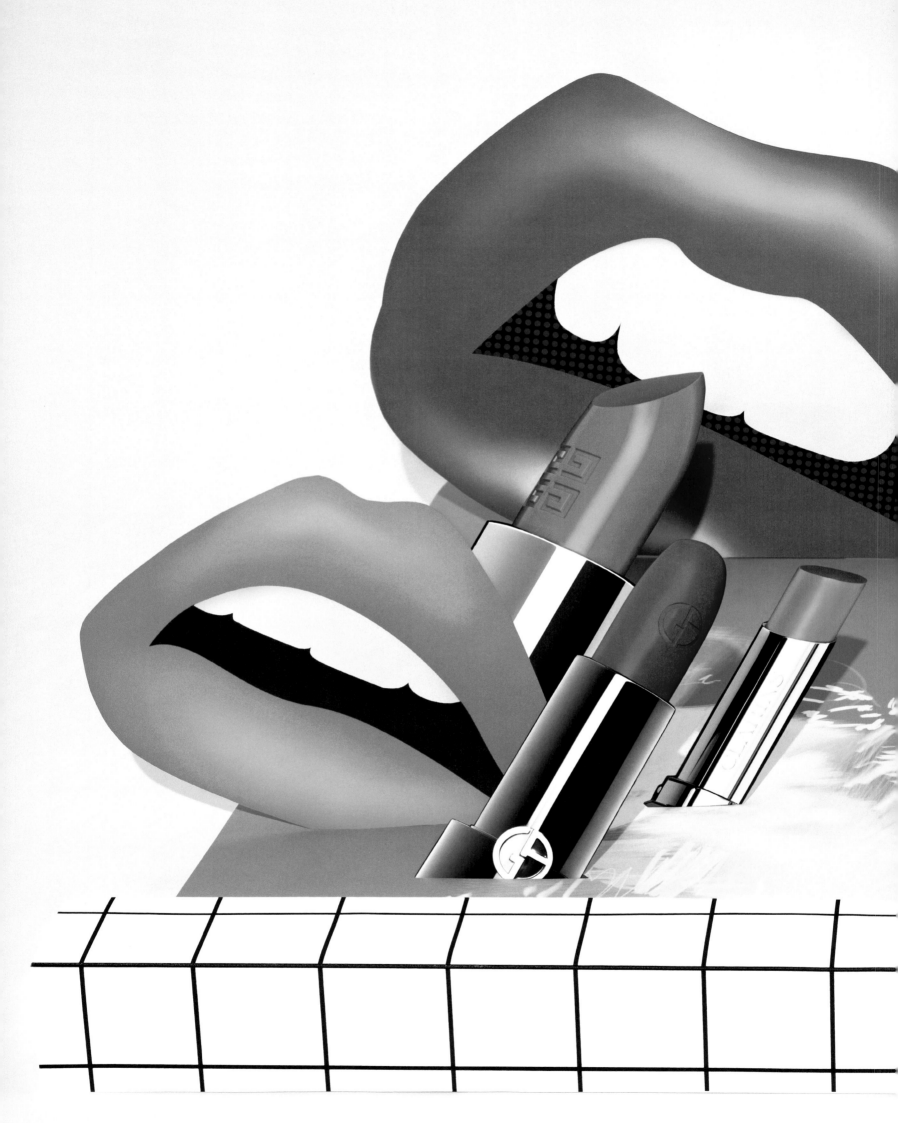

Photography | Set Design | Styling STILLS & STROKES

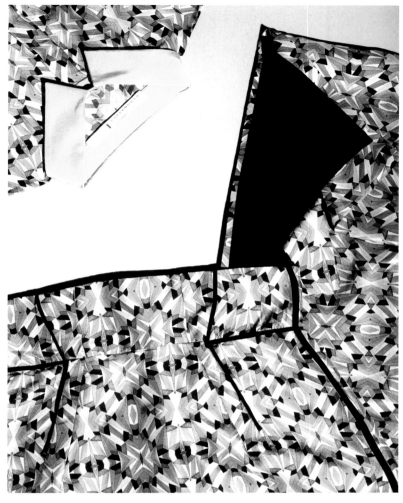

Editorial Project for TUSH   Photography | Styling | Set Design   STILLS & STROKES

out. We find it fascinating to experiment with the ways in which people perceive pictures, but also to explore the manifold ways in which they can be produced."

They have photographed products and then printed out the photo to be photographed again, like in their wonderfully Wesselmannian lipstick still life for *Interview* magazine. They replaced paper sets with broken mirrors for a recent feature for *Noah* magazine. Most of the time, however, product and paper set coexist, like two types of realities whose mingling establishes a lively exchange—both in the picture and on set, where Homann and Vorbeck engage in a ping pong process, or more precisely in a process of runaround ping pong, as they tend to roam around the table to put products and patterns into proper perspective. "Compared to digital compositions done on a computer, our analog setups allow us to walk around compositions, view things from various angles and intervene physically and collaboratively. We really work things out together on set, argue about angles and move elements of composition around. Oftentimes, that creates this sort of spur-of-the-moment, spontaneous energy that you usually don't have a lot doing still lifes," Hohman says.

The cats and dogs Stills & Strokes have recently photographed for a feature for *Tush* magazine surely had some spontaneous moments up in their furry sleeves, but despite all the fun they had shooting pets, the duo still prefers lifeless subjects. People have asked them, here and there, whether photographing human models would not be the natural next step. But they replied saying no. They like to work on their own and build paper sets in perfect privacy, removed from the business's hustle and bustle. Both paper and products have more patience than people. So for now, Stills & Strokes stay still. Which is, in their case, far from doing nothing.

Editorial Project for MIXT(E)   Photography   VINCENT GAPAILLARD

Styling   LILLY MARTHE EBENER   Set Design   MARILYN PERROD | JONATHAN BEY

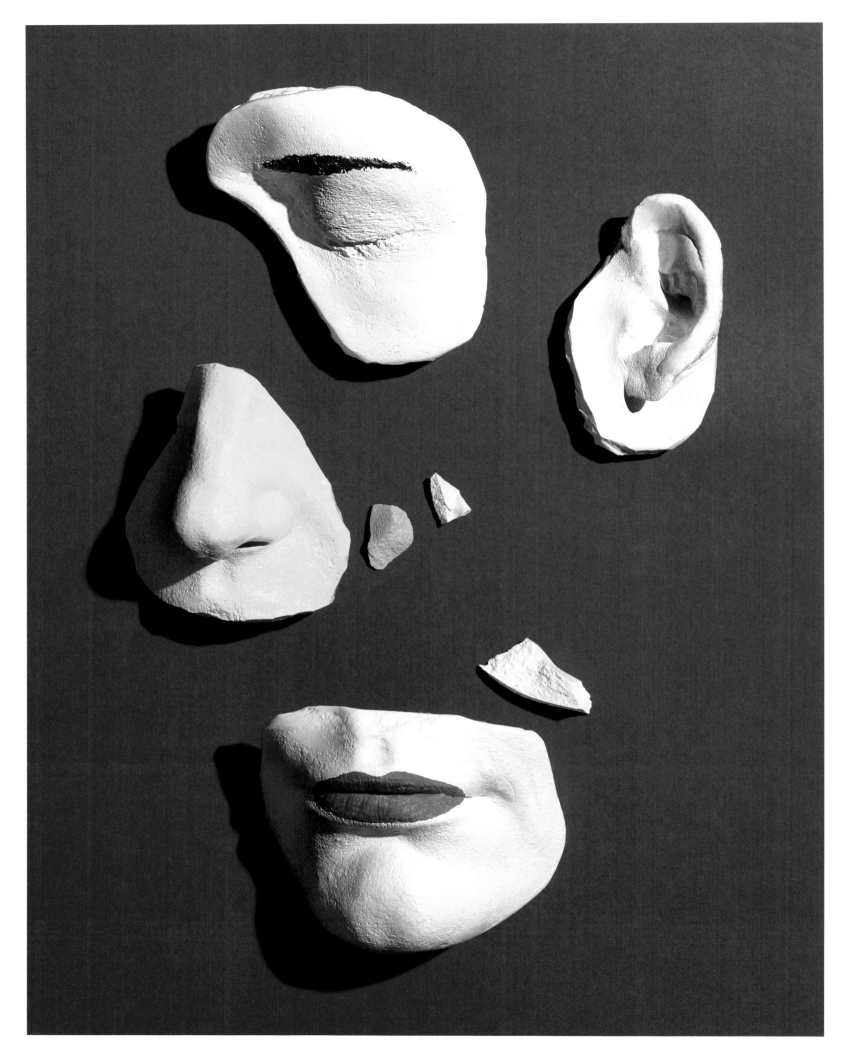

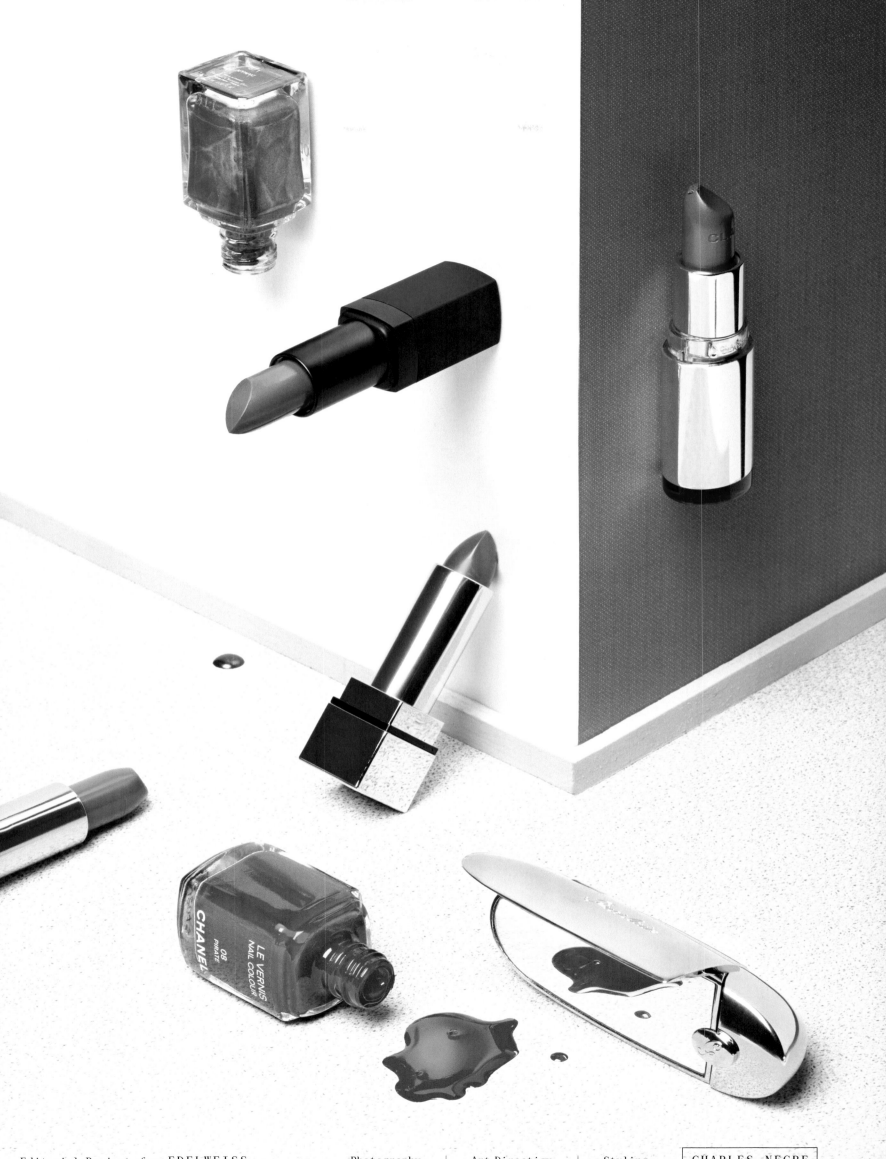

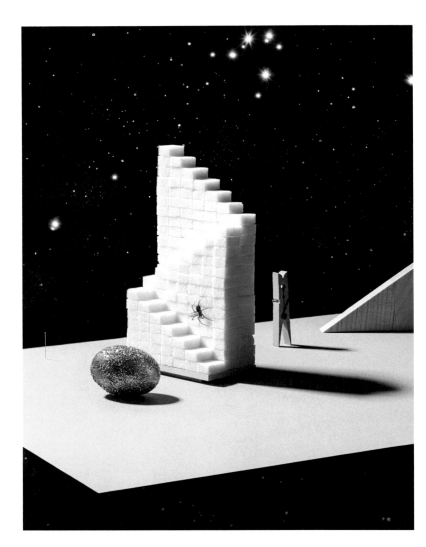

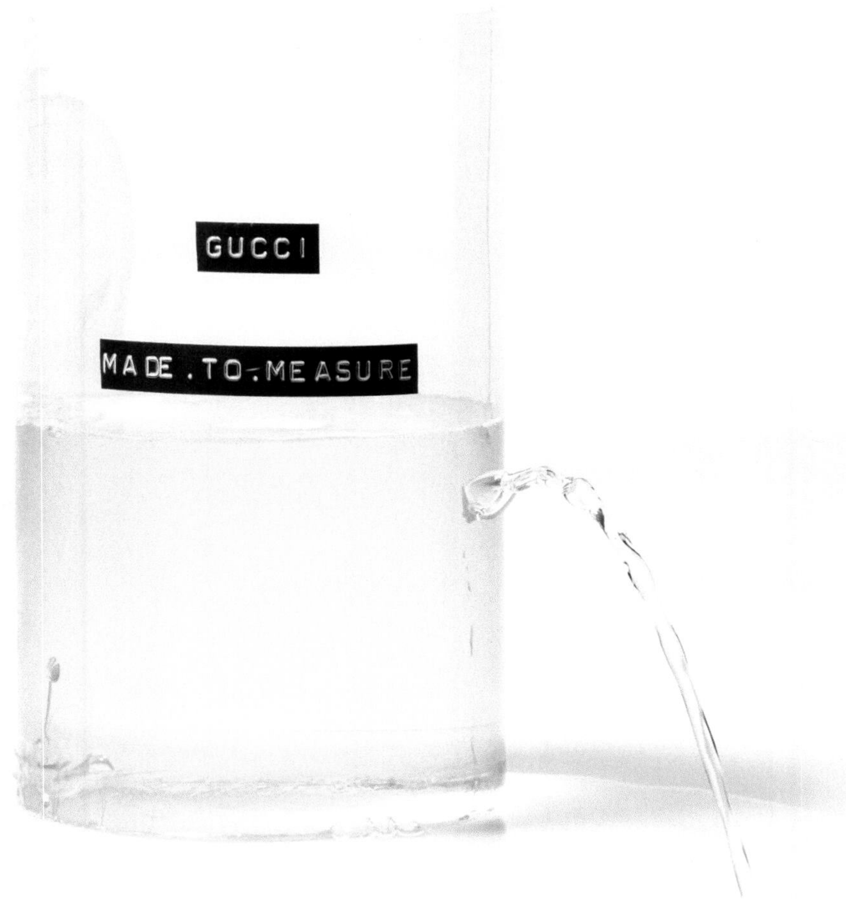
GUCCI
MADE.TO-MEASURE

Personal Project

Photography | Set Design

CARL KLEINER

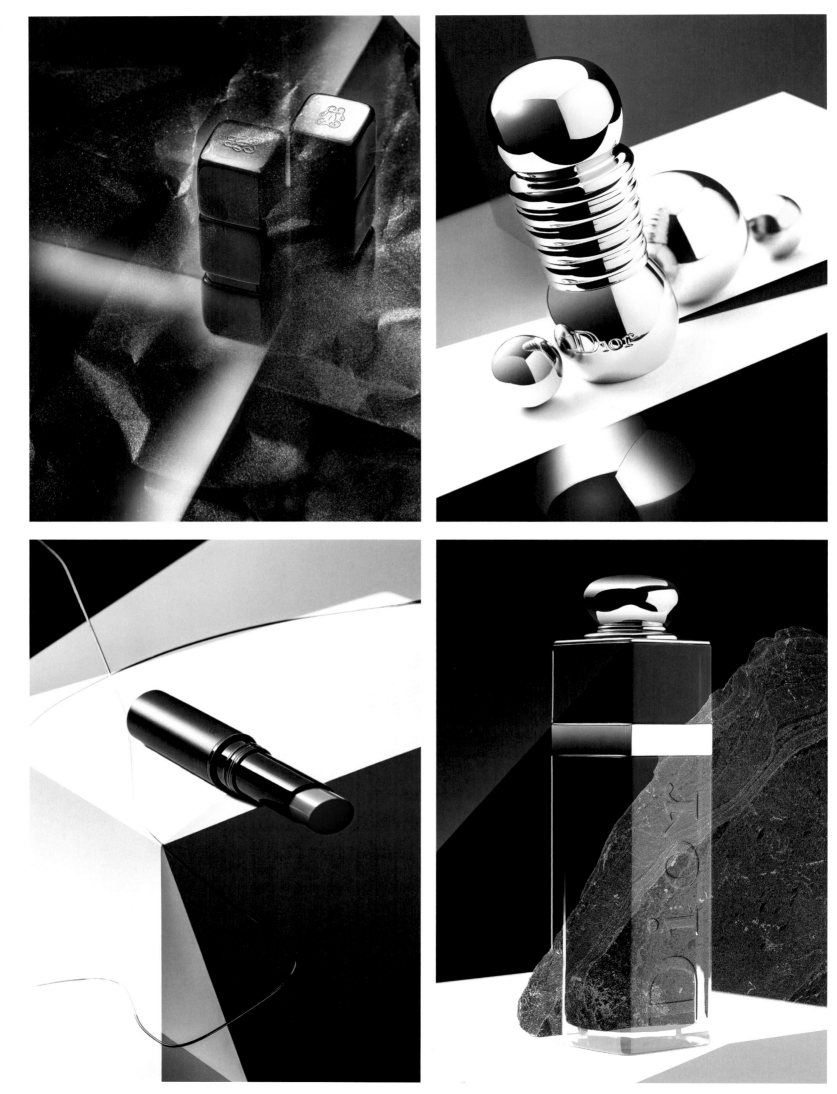

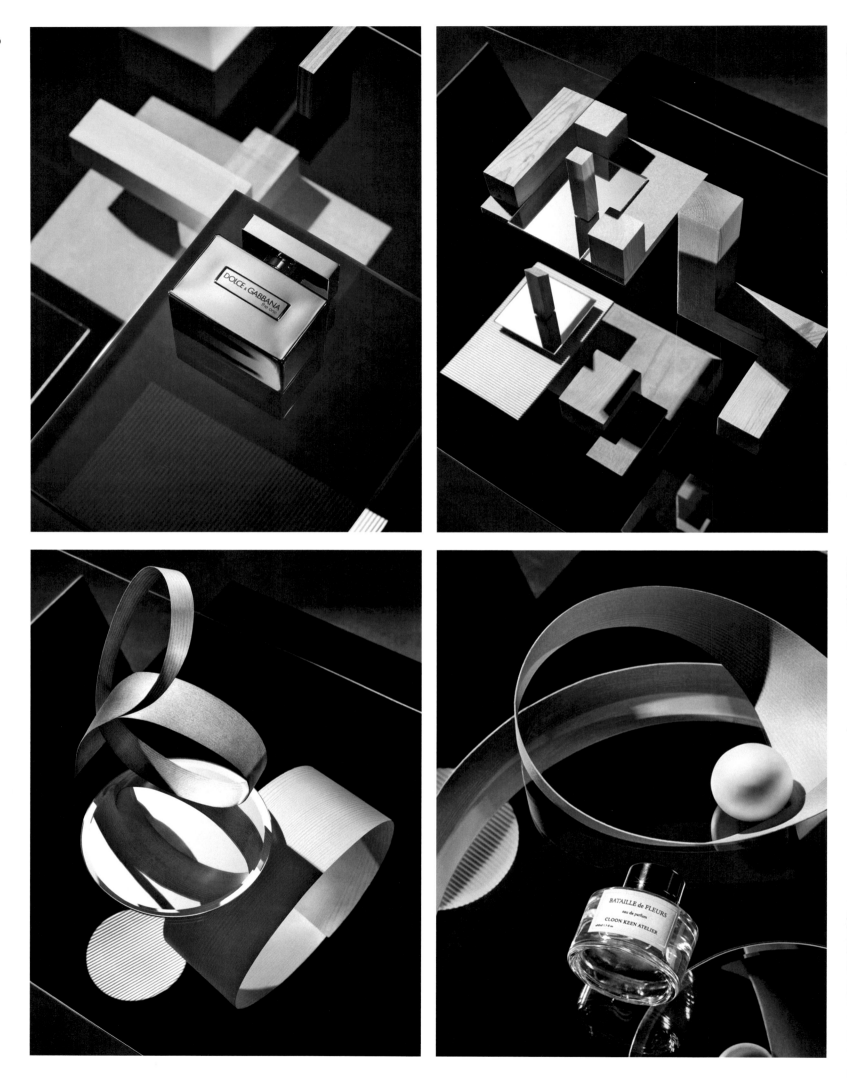

Personal Project   Photography | THOMAS BROWN | Art Direction | ROBERT STOREY |

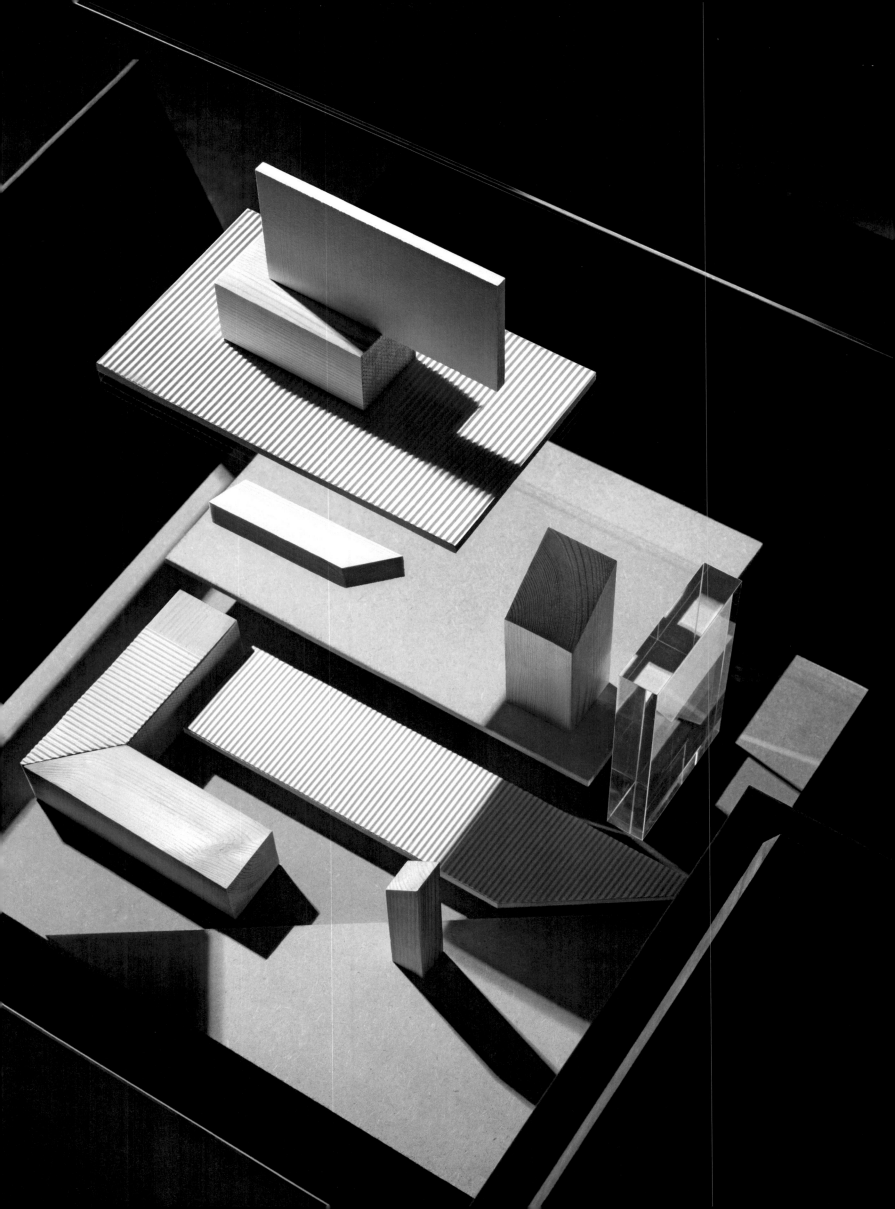

Photography   DAN TOBIN SMITH

Personal Project   Photography   PAUL LEPREUX   Art Direction | Set Design   ROMAIN LENANCKER

Personal Project   Photography   JAN BURWICK   Styling   CHRISTOPH HIMMEL

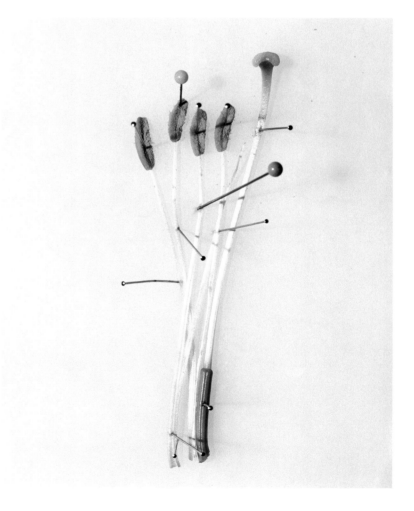

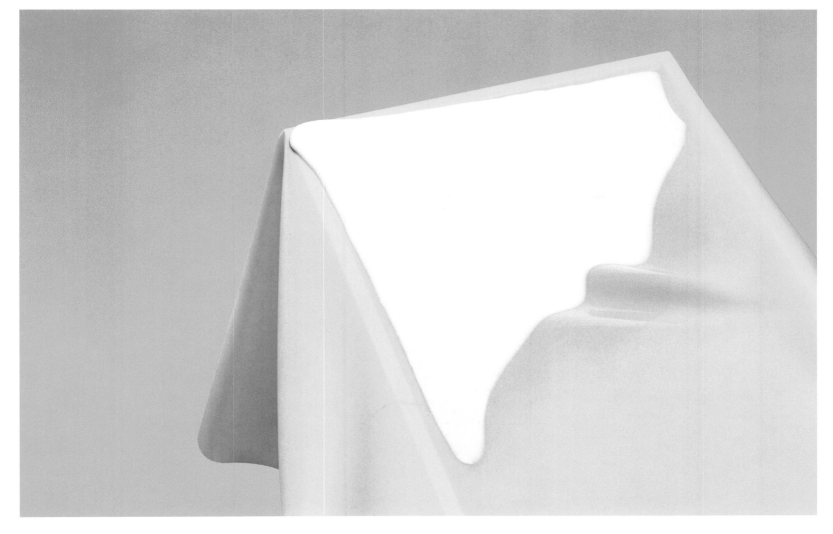

Editorial Project for VERITIES   Photography   MICHAEL BODIAM   Styling | Set Design   SARAH PARKER

Photography   MICHAEL BAUMGARTEN   Styling   CHRISTIANE JUERGENSEN

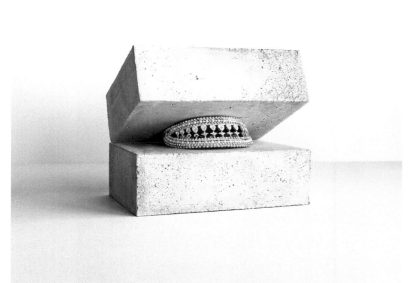

Photography | Art Direction | Set Design BENOIT PAILLEY Styling INES FENDRI

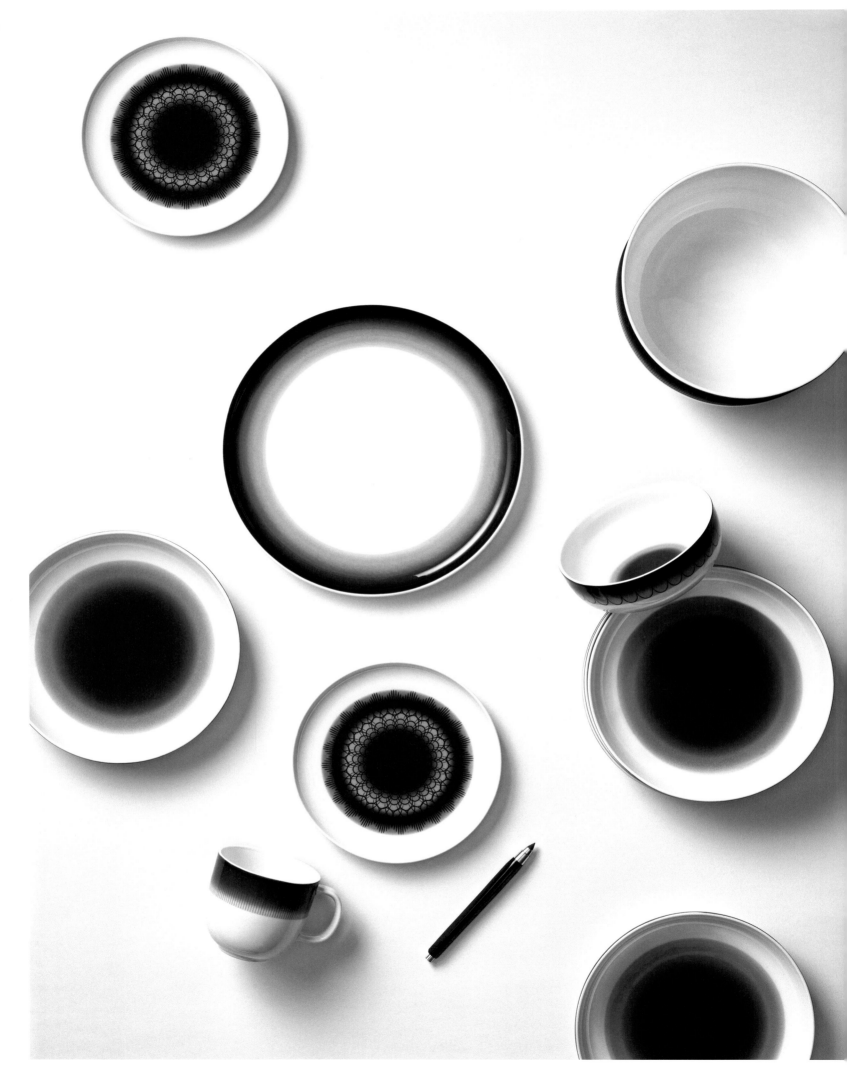

Corporate Project for RÖRSTRAND

Photography | BOHMAN + SJÖSTRAND | Art Direction | EBBA BLOMGREN | Styling | LOTTA AGATON |

Photography   BLOMMERS SCHUMM

Photography | Art Direction   LENA C. EMERY   Styling   RAQUEL GARCIA

SARAH PARKER

Set Design

Styling

|

MICHAEL BODIAM

Photography

Editorial Project for THE TELEGRAPH LUXURY

Personal Project

Photography

THOMAS POPINGER

Editorial Project for M LE MAGAZINE DU MONDE

Photography JOSS MCKINLEY Styling YANN LECORCHE Floral Design PIERRE BANCHEREAU

Editorial Project for ELLE GERMANY   Photography   PAUL LEPREUX   Styling   KATHRIN SEIDEL

Photography   VINCENT GAPAILLARD   Styling   MAYA ZEPINIC   Set Design   MARCEL VAN DOORN

Editorial Project for FRENCH REVUE DU MODES   Photography   THOMAS DE MONACO

Corporate Publishing Project for AIR FRANCE MADAME

Photography VINCENT GAPAILLARD Styling HERMIONE HARBAS Set Design RONAN TEISSÈDRE

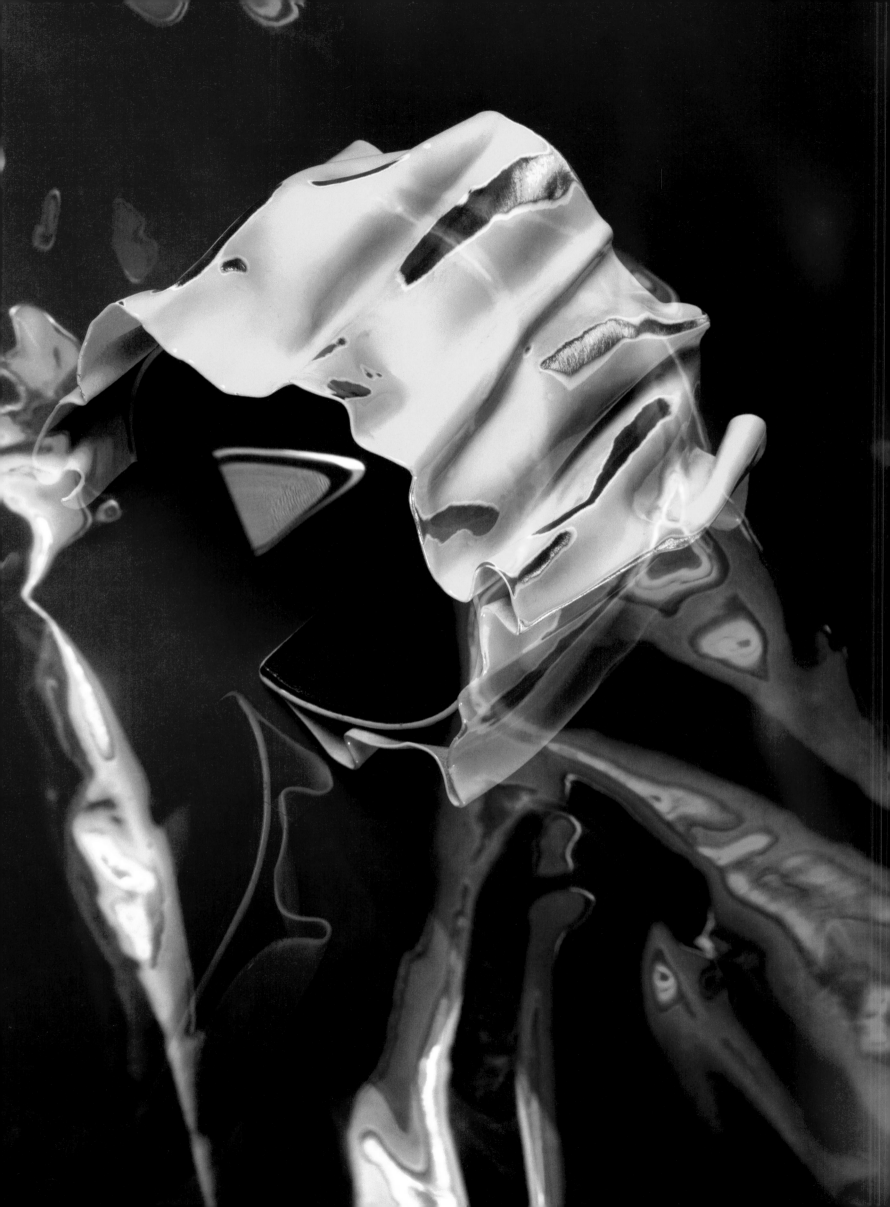

Editorial Project for ANOTHER   Photography | Art Direction | Styling   CHARLES NEGRE

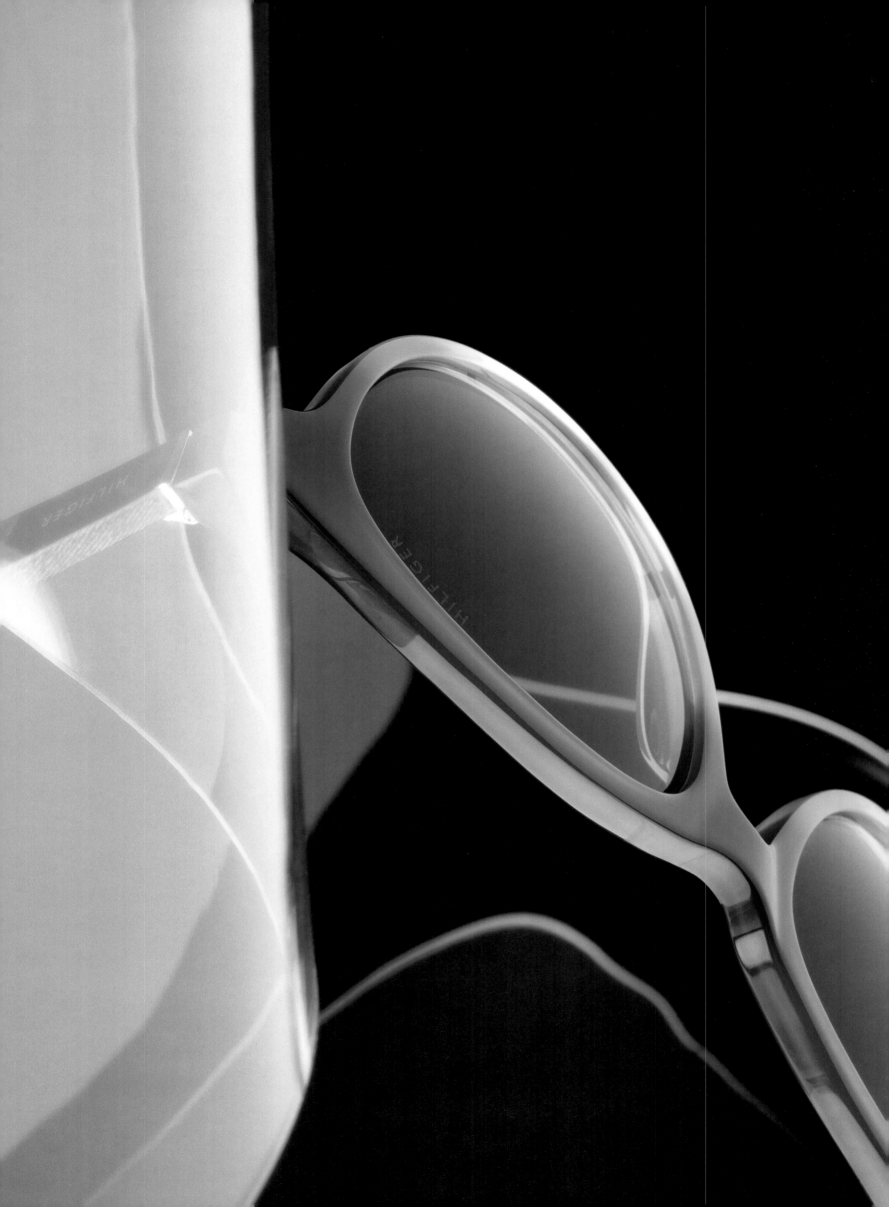

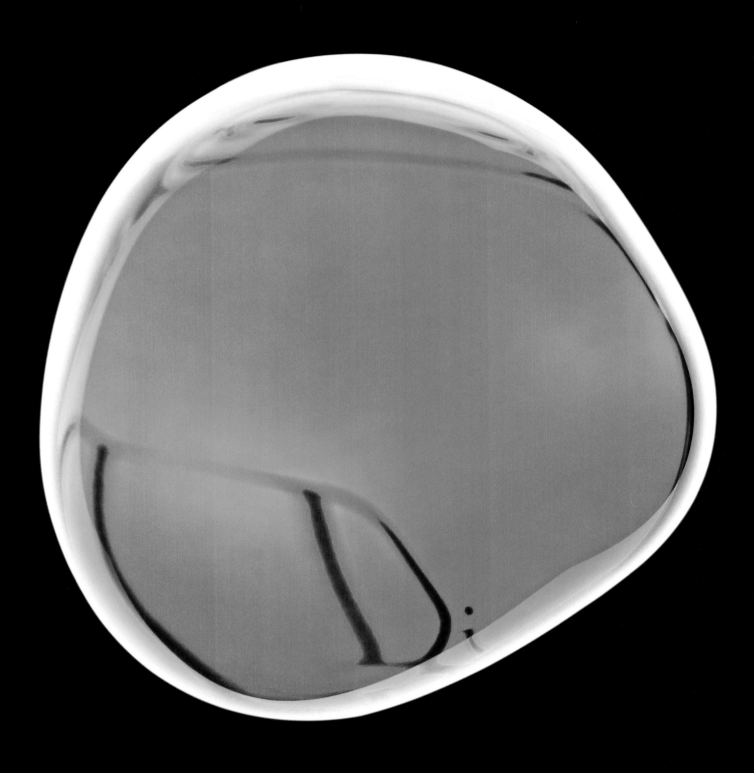

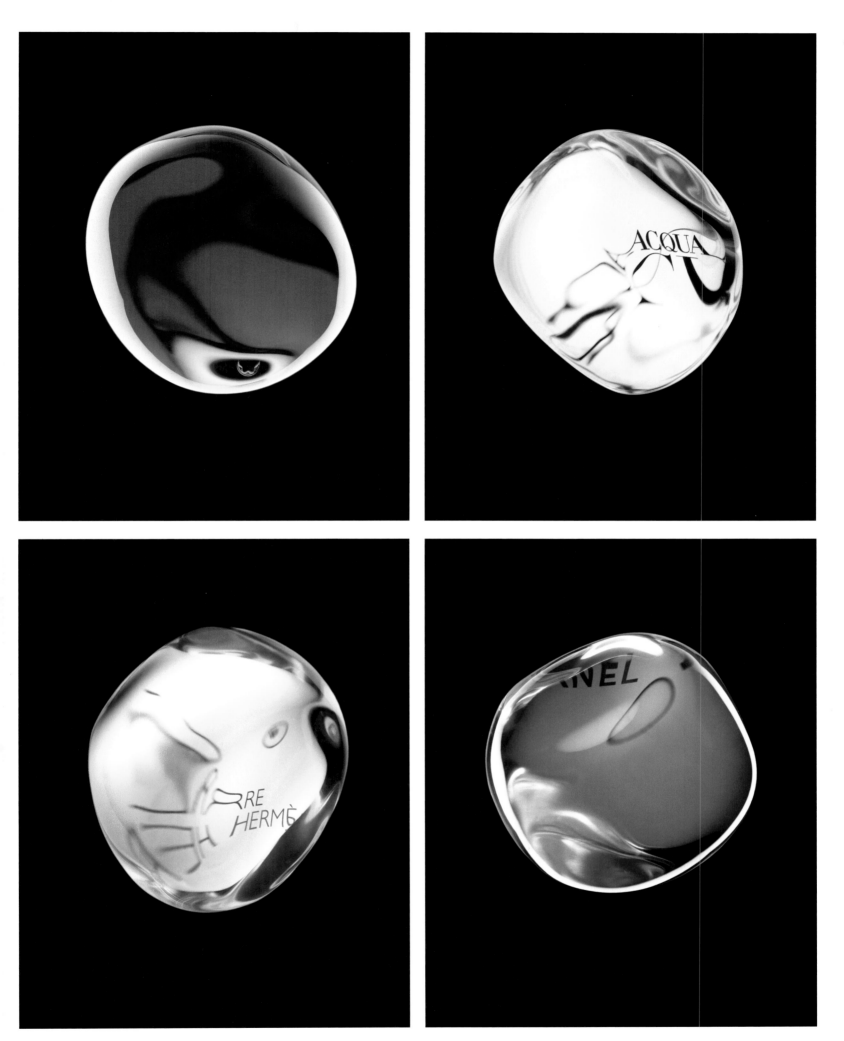

Photography PAUL LEPREUX Set Design | Art Direction ROMAIN LANEACKER

Advertising Project for COMME DES GARÇONS   Photography | Art Direction | Styling   CHARLES NEGRE

Corporate Project for PANTONE   Photography   AARON TILLEY   Art Direction   SANDY MACLENNAN

Corporate Project for ABSOLUT WODKA   Photography   BLOMMERS SCHUMM

Editorial Project for   FANTASTIC MAN   Photography   BLOMMERS SCHUMM

Personal Project

Photography | JESS BONHAM | Art Direction | JESS BONHAM | ANNA LOMAX | Styling | ANNA LOMAX

FEATURE: <u>METZ + RACINE</u>

Metz + Racine's still lifes live for the moment. Not for the mere pleasures of the present or the split second that may account for a snapshot's success, but rather for the moment almost missed. Seemingly slightly off-schedule, many of Metz + Racine's compositions capture the "right before" or the "right after." Real suspense, they appear to argue, resides in juxtapositions between disparate objects, between an act and its imminent instance, or between the present and the point it just passed.

Editorial Project for NUMÉRO HOMME   Photography   METZ + RACINE   Set Design   HERVÉ SAUVAGE

"Some objects seem to be moved by invisible forces," Metz + Racine say, and from time to time, things seem to slip or fall out the frames of their still lifes, which, as they note, are in fact "not so still." Indeed, one often finds signs of life and lapsed time in their images of toppled jars or crumpled clothes. Some clearly imply that someone has just left the picture, letting the viewer occasionally catch a glimpse of a hand or a leg. Some situations seem casual while others seem to be superbly staged, but all are imbued with a hint of human presence.

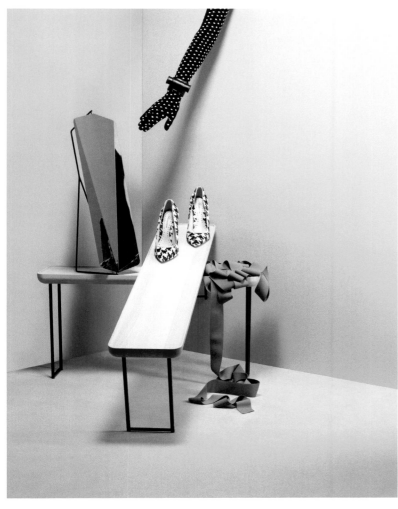

Set Design | Furniture Styling HERVÉ SAUVAGE Fashion Styling STORNY + MISERICORDIA

Editorial Project for PIZZA

Photography   METZ + RACINE   Art Direction   ARABESCHI DI LATTE   Food Styling   FRANCESCA SARTI

Metz + Racine is an established photographic partnership between Barbara Metz and Eve Racine based in London. Metz is originally from Germany, Racine from Switzerland, but the two met whilst studying photography at the London College of Communication. Their collaboration began while Eve was continuing her studies at the Royal College of Art for a masters and Metz had just started to freelance. "The experience of working as a team and the shared taste made this first step very organic. We didn't have a business plan but we enjoyed working together and very soon couldn't imagine doing anything else."

Barbara Metz and Eve Racine are united by a fascination for the unexpected life that lies within objects. For them, all products have a personality that is merely waiting to be brought to life in an image. Metz + Racine mostly shoot luxury products, and that is not only because they enjoy taking pictures of things they like: "Brands like Louis ▷

Editorial Project for TUSH

Photography | METZ + RACINE | Art Direction | Set Design | ROMAIN LENANCKER

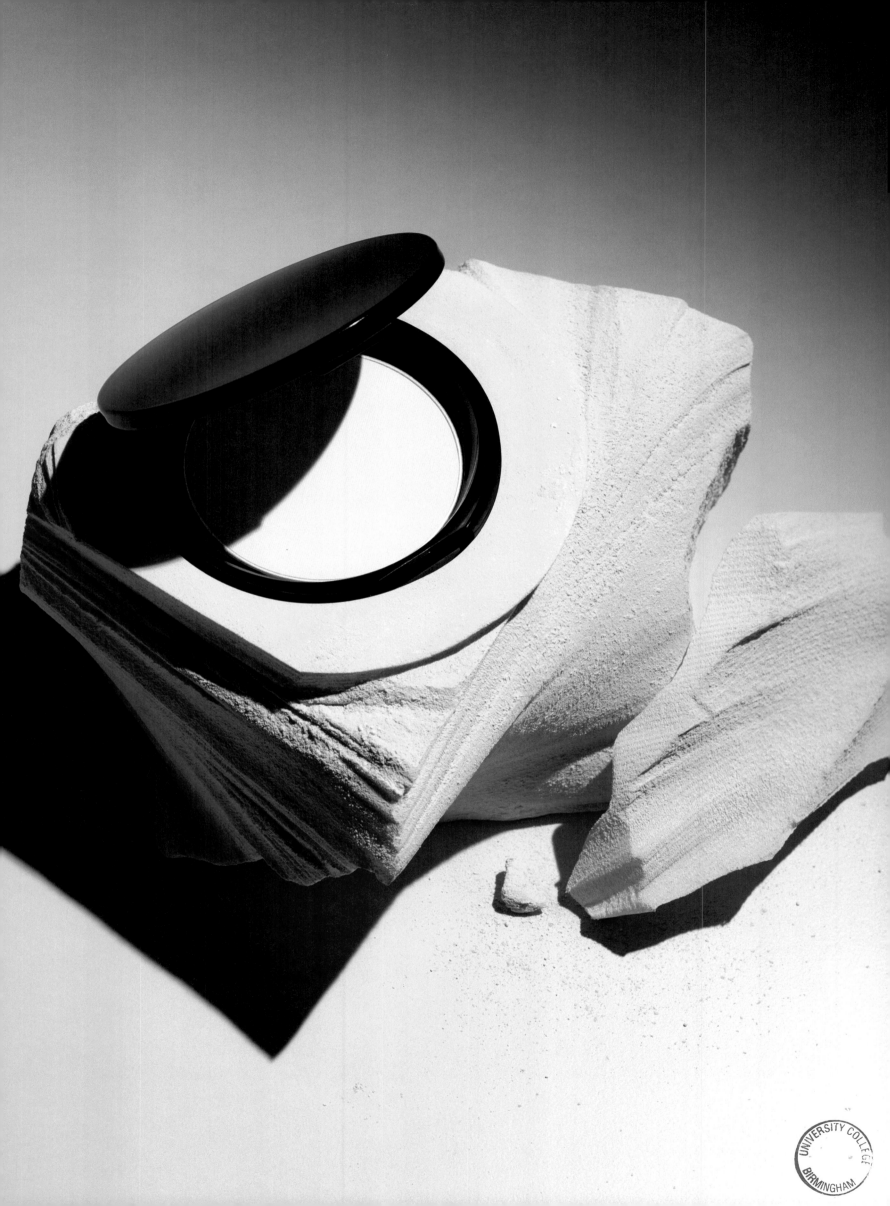

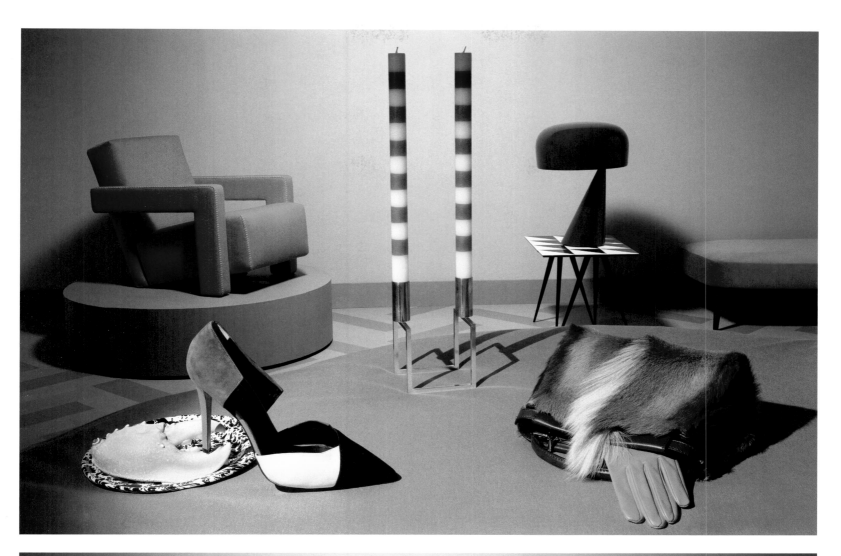

Set Design | Furniture Styling JANINA PEDAN Fashion Styling MADELEINE ØSTLIE

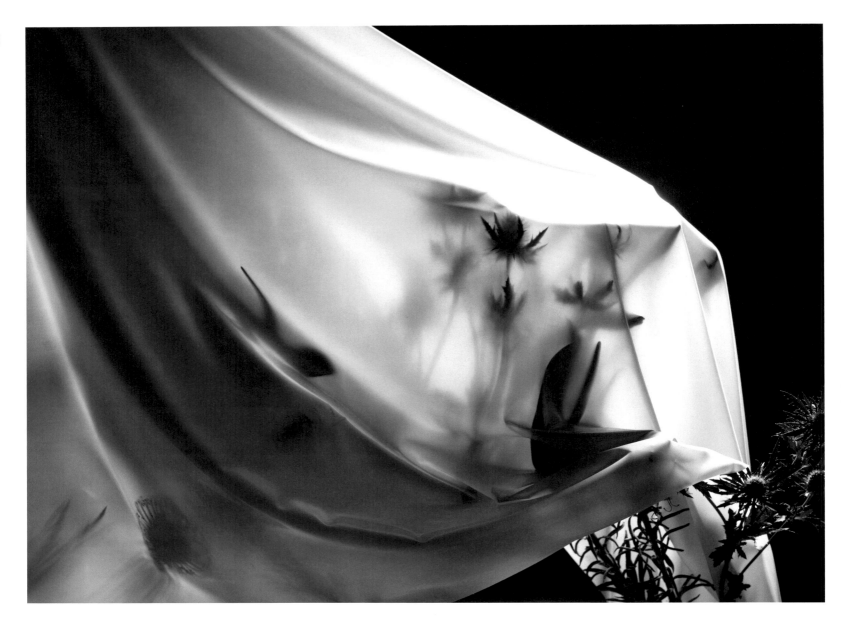

Editorial Project for VIEWPOINT

Photography | METZ + RACINE | Styling | JANE HOWARD | Set Design | DAVID WHITE |

Vuitton, Hermès, and Chanel understand our visual language, which is sophisticated and playful. In turn, we believe we understand the needs of big luxury brands and share some of their core values, like craftsmanship and a love for details."

Despite their affinity for luxury labels, Metz + Racine switch between big commercial jobs and smaller editorial ones with joy and astounding ease. They enjoy alternating between table tops, bigger sets, and spacious installations. They welcome the contrast between elaborate fashion shoots that involve large teams and numerous sets on the one hand and editorial commissions on the other. The latter allow Metz + Racine to develop "moods and moments" from scratch and to control all details of the production. The level of precision remains the same, regardless of the application or scale of a project, they say, but large sets always involve a loss of control, so it is important to learn to let go.

"Obviously, one needs to be organized and have a good idea of what needs to be achieved in order to be able to shoot several images a day, which is why we plan any production as well as we can. However, we have come to a point where we are happy to explore ideas while we shoot." There must be space for creativity on set, they say, sometimes simply because many things work in a sketch but not in natura. Sometimes images need an intuitive twist. And some of the most interesting things happen intuitively, so they try their best to remain receptive throughout the process, especially when working with bigger teams. ▷

140

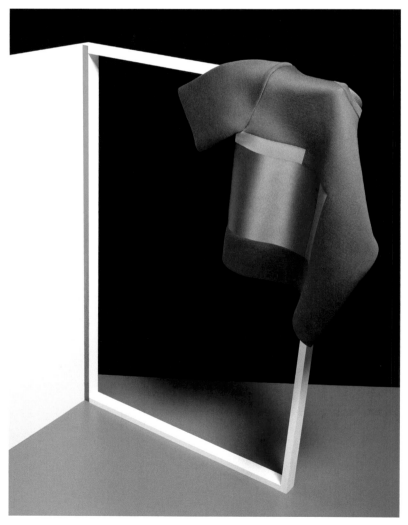

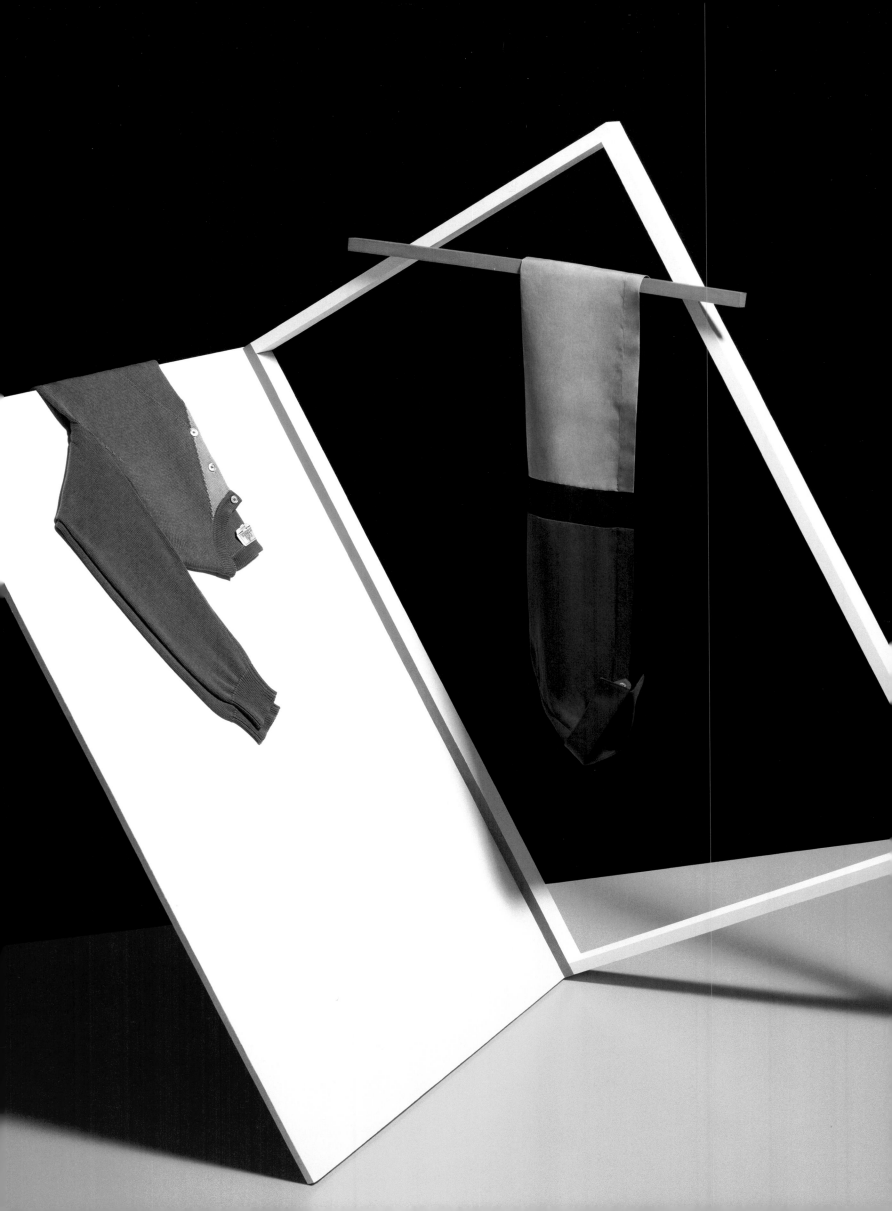

Photography   METZ + RACINE   Styling   CLÉMENCE CAHU   Set Design   GEORGINA PRAGNELL

Since the establishment of their photography partnership back in 2000, Metz + Racine have built up a considerable network of stylists and set designers they trust and enjoy working with, while remaining on the lookout for new creatives for potential collaborations. They used to do a lot of styling themselves in the early days of their careers and still treasure the experience of working in a hands-on manner, developing sets autonomously and sometimes quite spontaneously. Yet at the same time, they value the energy that joint ventures bring. "To stay creative under commercial pressure requires a relaxed atmosphere," they say. "Clients are often under a lot of pressure and we like to minimize it for them. We take our work and clients very seriously but not necessarily ourselves!" The lovable lightness of their approach resonates in Metz + Racine's images, which counter rough commercial realities with charming colors and carefully crafted compositions.

"We strongly believe in the artistic approach and in taking the time it takes to arrive at an interesting image." Time, to Metz + Racine, is as vital as creative headspace: if they do not have enough, they are not able to produce visuals that stand out, as they see it. But as most of Metz + Racine's recent commissions come from the luxury sector, they are lucky enough to have clients who give them relatively generous timeframes and financial resources to materialize elaborate ideas. Especially in light of the rapid pace of contemporary image culture, time is a rare luxury in itself.

Today, products are symbols of prestige and photographs proofs of presence. According to Metz + Racine, "it is amazing to see the need for people to share their experiences through photographs." Yet it is also somewhat dizzying to witness the need for speed in their production—the rapid design and distribution of images oftentimes results in a decrease in quality. "A lot of contemporary photography has a tendency to look and feel similar," note Metz + Racine. "The pictures that will really survive through time are mostly those that have a certain stillness and perfection to them. One doesn't necessarily need to see the work that has gone into them, but get a sense of balance. We like the idea that at first glance our still lifes feel classical and only upon closer inspection

Editorial Project for MIXT(E)

reveal a modern touch. The classic still has not lost its poetic appeal, and we believe it is a very exciting time for the genre. But it is also good to see things evolving."

Constantly on their toes to further develop their own style, Metz + Racine have recently started working with moving images, which, to them, is the most natural progression. "We enjoy the challenges the medium brings, especially as compared to working with still lives. Expanding outside the confines of photography, the story continues—it is part of an ongoing evolution." Maybe some of their films will pick up on the slightly off-moments portrayed in their stills…. But would we really want to find out what has happened before, or what comes after? Perhaps we should leave those fluttering moments alone to remain intact.

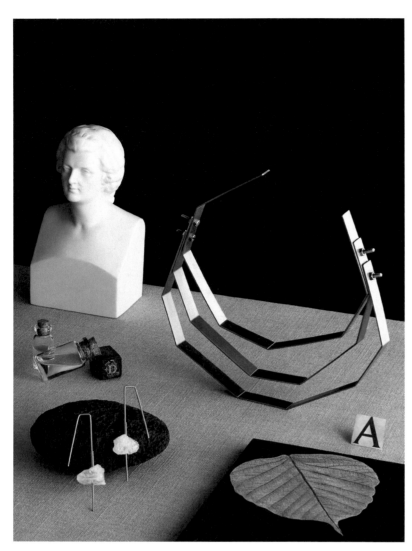

Corporate Project for MALIN HENNINGSSON JEWELERY   Photography   CHRISTOFFER DARKALS

Editorial Project for ALVAR   Photography | Art Direction   BAKER & EVANS   Styling   SARAH PARKER

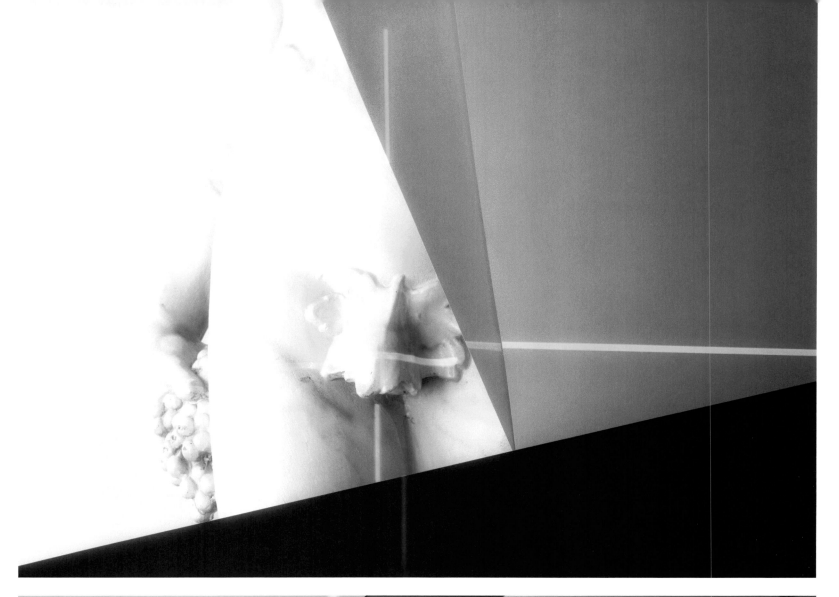

Editorial Project for SPIEGEL   Photography   OLIVER SCHWARZWALD   Styling   ELENA MORA

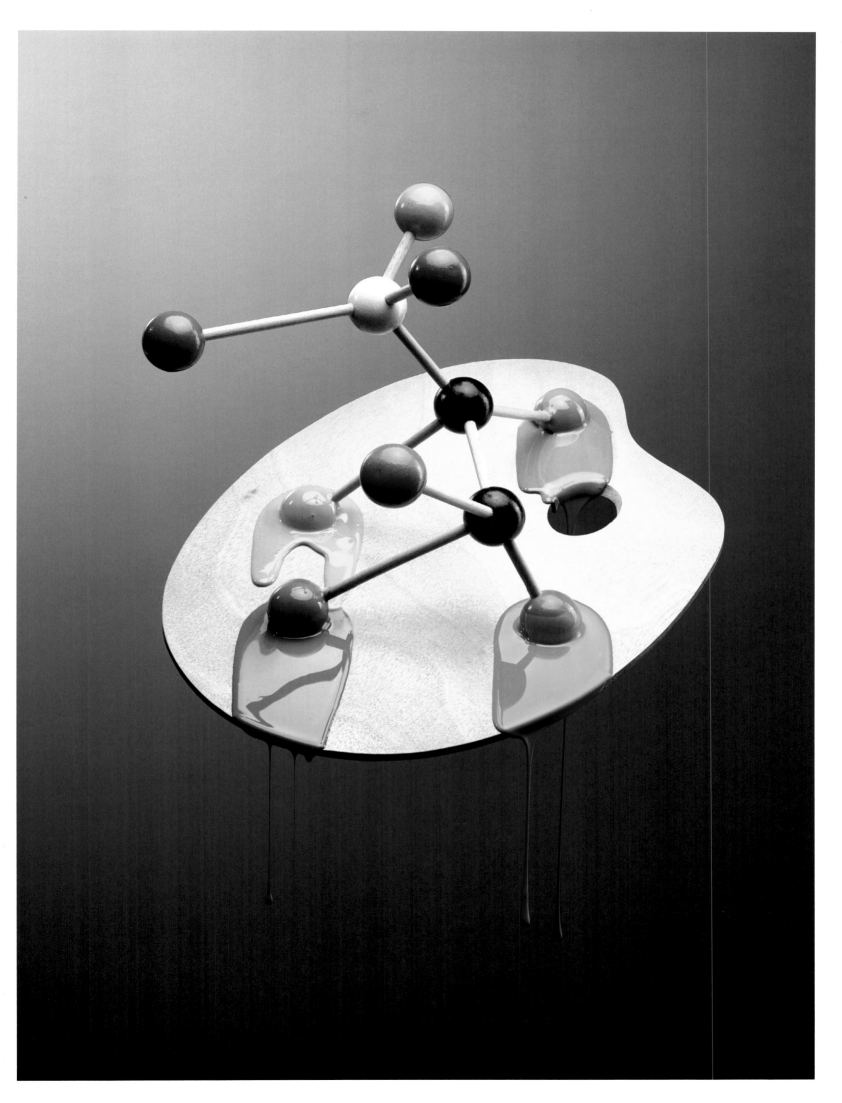

Editorial Project for THE ATLANTIC   Photography   SAM HOFMAN   Styling | Set Design   KYLE BEAN

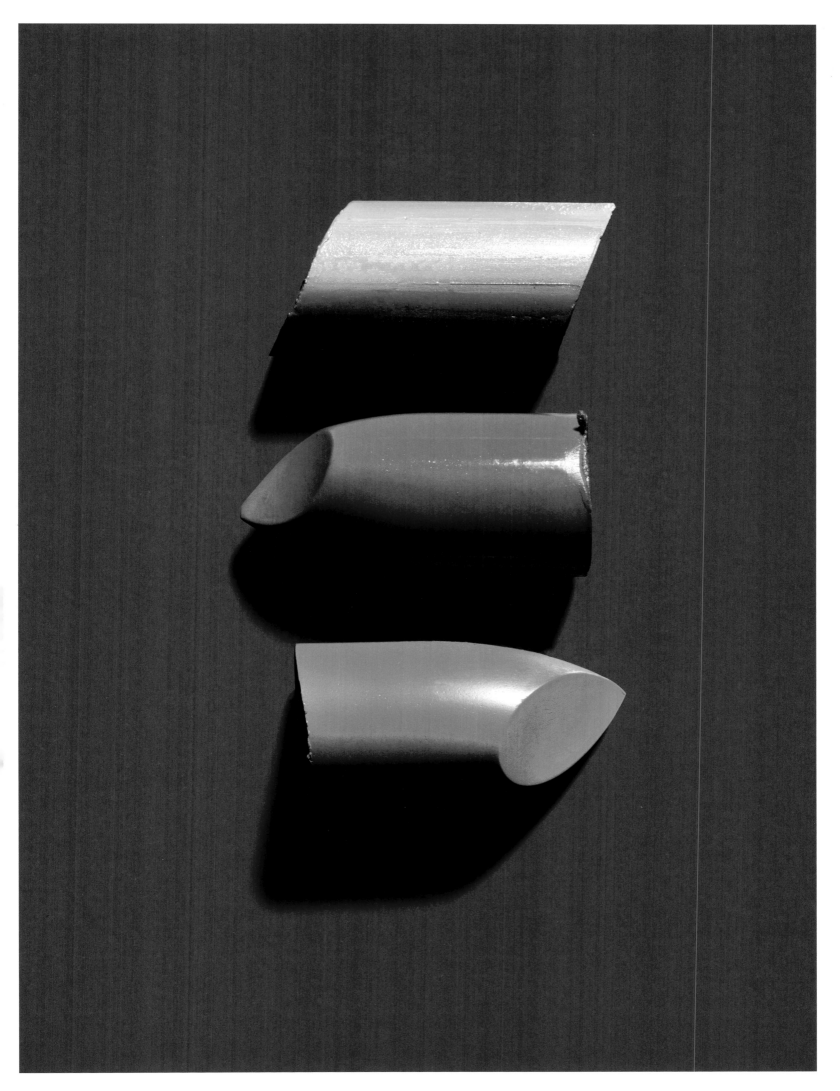

Photography | Styling KENJI AOKI

Corporate Project for ULF ROLLOFF   Photography   BOHMAN + SJÖSTRAND   Art Direction   PETER HERRMANN

Personal Project

Photography | Art Direction | Styling

AKATRE

Editorial Project for ZEIT WISSEN

Photography

HAW-LIN SERVICES

Personal Project   Photography   ATTILA HARTWIG   Styling   NINA LEMM

Corporate Project for VAN LAACK

Photography   KLAUS ALTEVOGT   Styling   ANKE LACHMUTH

Editorial Project for M LE MAGAZINE DU MONDE

Photography | Concept | Set Design | MIRKA LAURA SEVERA | Styling | ALINE DE BEAUCLAIRE |

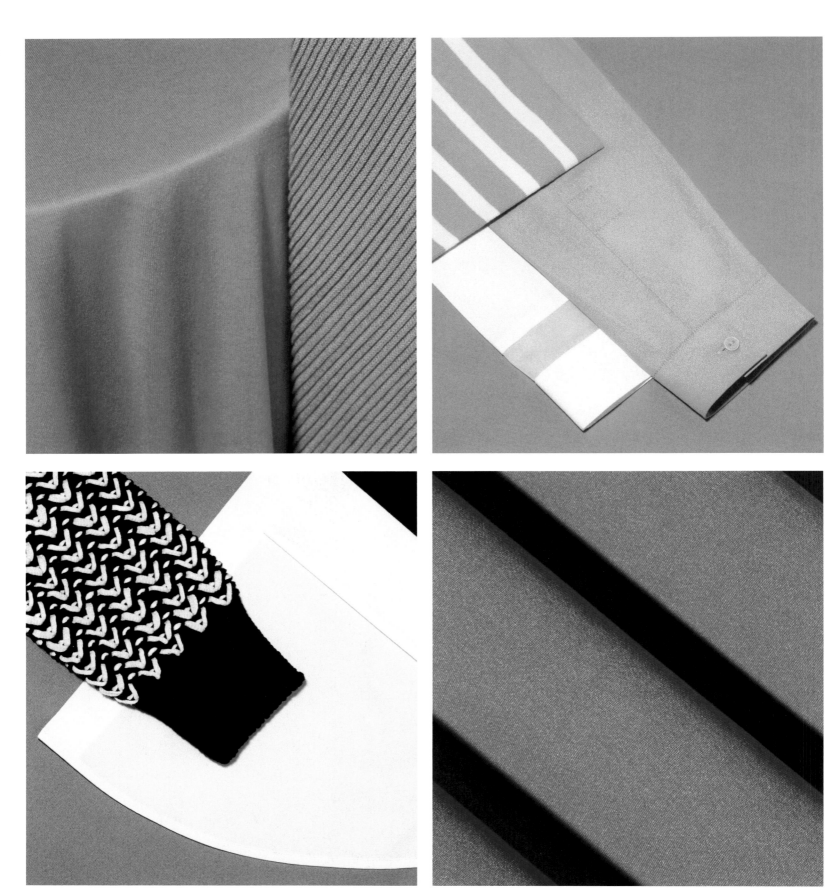

Corporate Project for COS   Photography | BAKER & EVANS | Styling | SARAH PARKER |

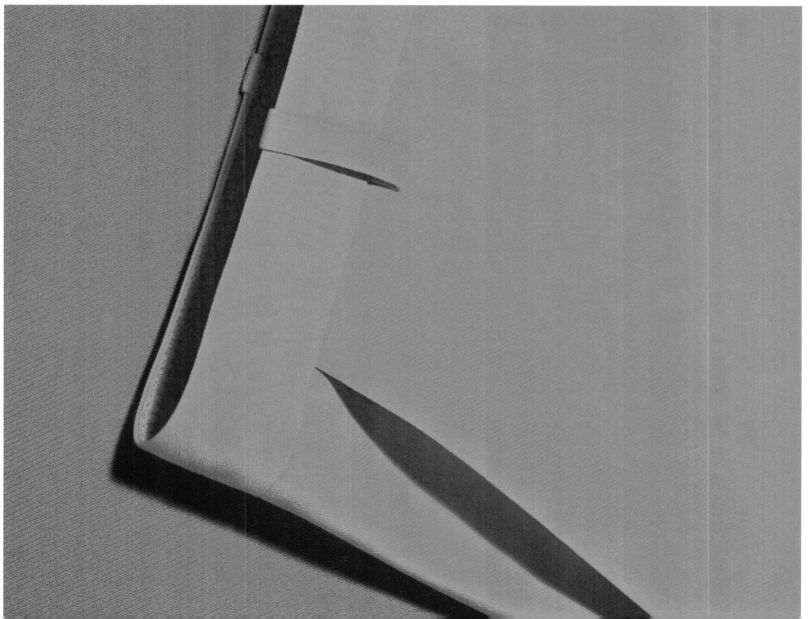

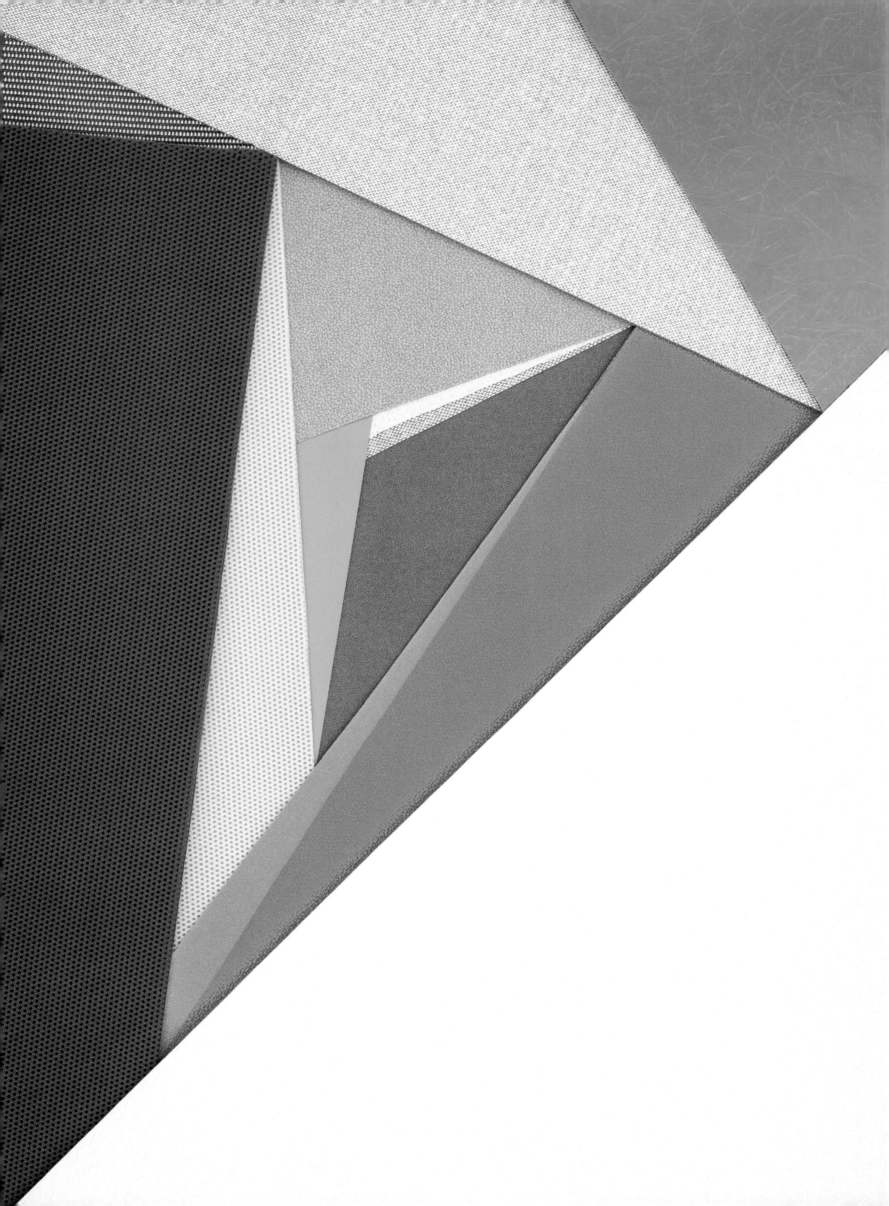

Corporate Project for HERMAN MILLER   Photography | Set Design   CARL KLEINER

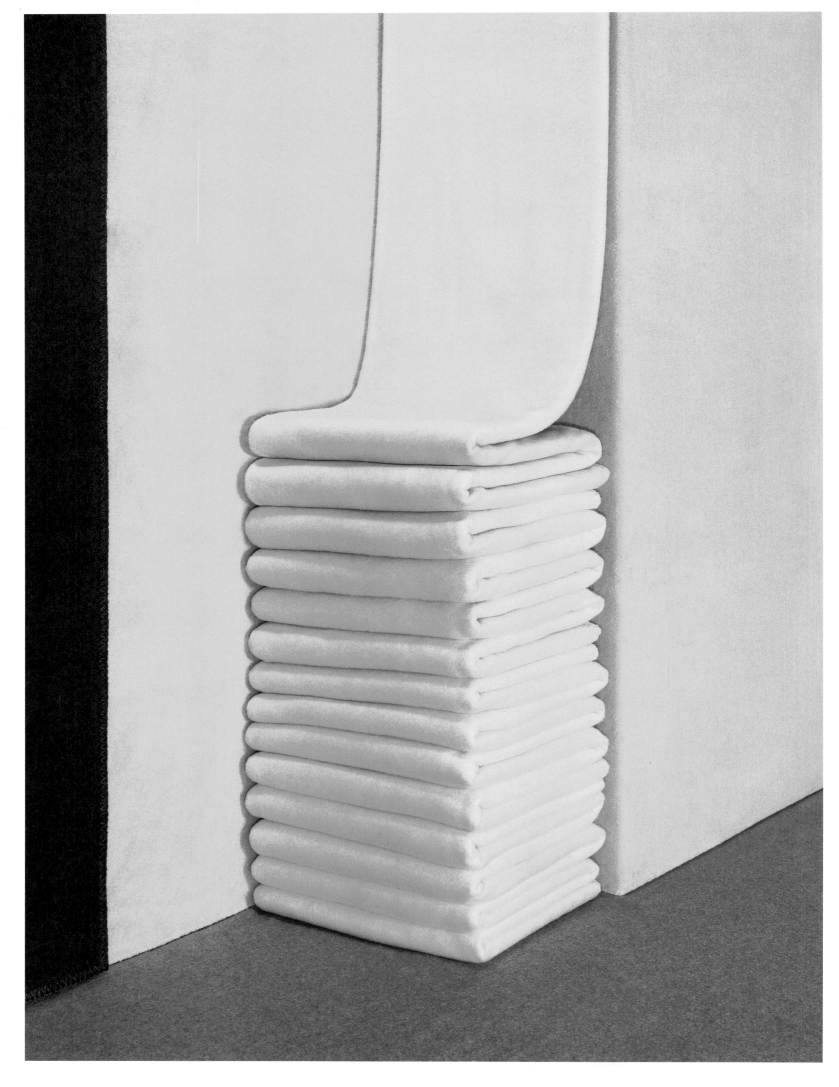

Corporate Project for JAG ZOEPRITZ   Photography | Art Direction | Set Design   MIRKA LAURA SEVERA

Corporate Project for RODEBJER   Photography | BOHMAN + SJÖSTRAND | Art Direction | MAJA KÖLQVIST |

Corporate Project for JMB JEWELLERY

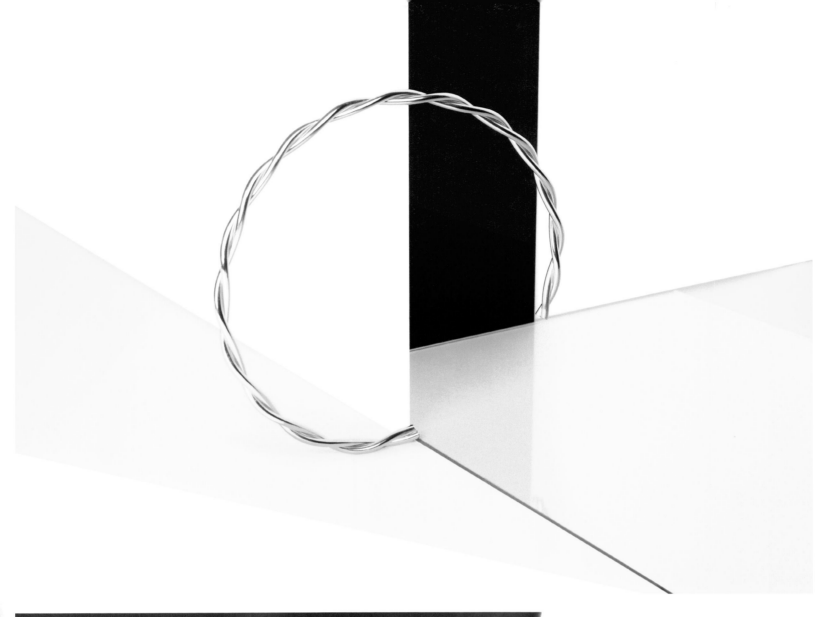

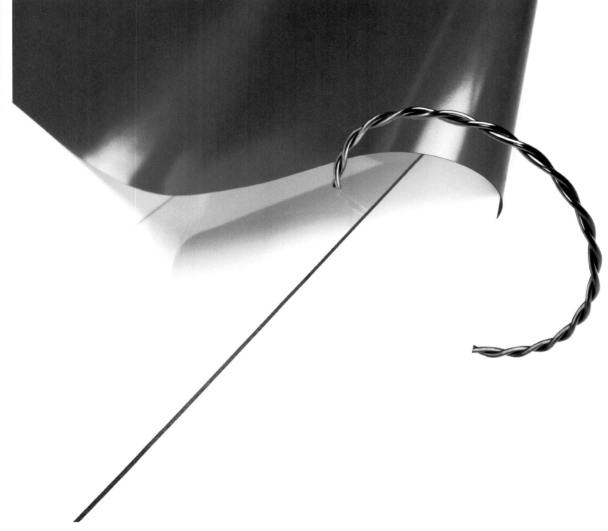

Photography | Art Direction | Set Design | GIULIA MUNARI | Styling | JORINDE MELINE BARKE

Corporate Project for ETIENNE GARACHON   Photography | Art Direction | Styling   CHARLES NEGRE

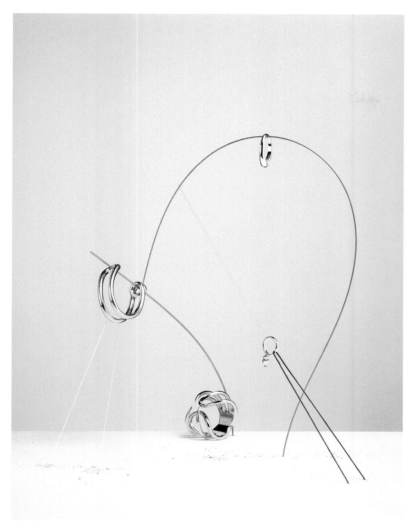
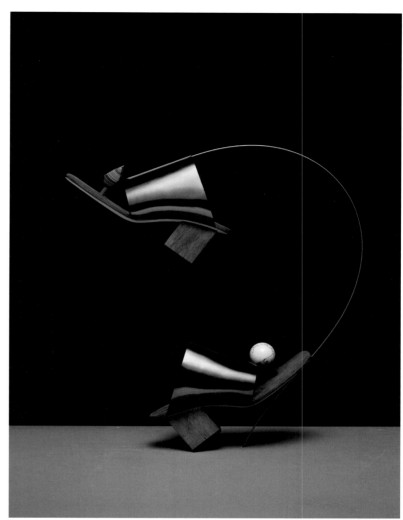
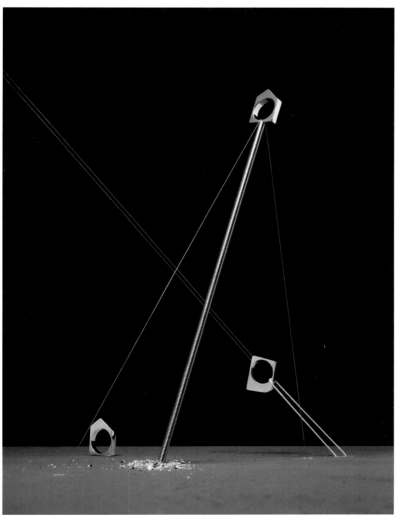

Editorial Project for ANOTHER   Photography   CARL KLEINER   Set Design   AGATA BELECEN

There is some sort of unsuspected life in each and every life-less object. In still life photography, the object takes the role of the protagonist and consequently becomes an actor. But few objects are fit to act without support—they need agents. Artists like Maurice Scheltens and Liesbeth Abbenes, who study structures and surfaces in order to, in their own words, "understand what all these things are trying to tell us," help objects be understood by putting them in proper perspective.

"Photography has the potential to reveal some-thing, to show us the unimagined side of things that is only visible from the point of view of the camera," Scheltens and Abbenes say. And viewed through their lens, some things look incredibly different indeed. They use perspective as a tool to take products apart, to deconstruct or dissect them. Drawing inspiration from the object itself, they focus in on its core features, the "building blocks of their composition," to steer us straight into the thick of things. Whether portraying fash-ion or furniture, Scheltens & Abbenes's pictures always reflect a keen interest in material properties and promote photography as a means to explore them.

"We are fascinated by how things are made, by anything that is carefully crafted, no matter the field," Liesbeth Abbenes notes. A graduate of the Gerrit Rietveld and Rijksacademy of Fine Arts in Amsterdam, Abbenes had worked on hand-embroidered wall tapestries before she met Maurice Scheltens, who had studied photography at the Royal Academy of Art in The Hague in the early nineties—a time when the still life was not very popular, which, in his view, only made it more interesting to specialize in. ▷

Publishing Project for MUSÉE DE LA MODE PARIS

Photography | Styling   SCHELTENS & ABBENES   Art Direction   OLIVIER SAILLARD

The two began working together back in 2002, and collaborations became more frequent after their separate studios were moved into the same building. In 2009, they physically connected their studio spaces and squeezed an ampersand in between their surnames. So, Scheltens & Abbenes was born. And with it, a prolific combination of competences that would open up unimagined possibilities on what a still life can be.

Scheltens & Abbenes's visual vocabulary is abstract and gloriously graphic. Working on the premise that all the products they photograph deserve a second look, they deliberately dazzle the onlooker with angles and arrangements that alienate or even obscure objects, rendering them abstract on the brink of recognition. Working on the threshold between illustration and interpretation, they sound out the "right" level of abstraction once on set, as it requires a sensibility they only begin to develop during the shoot.

In contrast to crowded fashion sets, Scheltens & Abbenes are shrouded in the creative silence of fertile concentration—a silence that is strongly perceptible in their pictures. "Most magazines are loud, packed with a lot of pictures and different image information," they say. "We wanted to see if we could create some sort of deafening silence." Featured in internationally acclaimed publications, their projects challenge familiar patterns of perception and thus indeed force us to pause.

While in the duo's early days clients would occasionally complain about a product being veiled by its visual presentation in Scheltens & Abbenes's work, companies now hire them precisely because of their experimental approach. It is thanks to their distinct signature style and their persistency in putting it out there that Scheltens & Abbenes have arrived at this stage. Unflinchingly following the unwritten rule to only take on projects that promise to reflect their ideals, they gained the grace of renowned clients like COS or the couture house Balenciaga, whose historic collections they photographed for the Musée de la Mode in Paris.

Too fragile to be transported, these fine garments forced Scheltens & Abbenes to shoot in the archive room, where the clothes are stored in special drawers that keep them dry and avoid temperature shifts. This is a rare example of the two creatives working outside of their Amsterdam studio, which they like to call their "lab"—a term that befits their laborious working method. "We feel fairly oblivious to the world, which asks for some sort of research attitude," they say, adding that the pictorial precision and meticulous make of their still lifes parallel that of old master paintings, with which they appear to have so little in common: "Looking at the way these painters celebrated their ▷

Editorial Project for THE GENTLEWOMAN   Photography | Styling   SCHELTENS & ABBENES

Photography | Styling SCHELTENS & ABBENES Art Direction JOP VAN BENNEKOM

Editorial Project for FANTASTIC MAN   Photography | Styling   SCHELTENS & ABBENES

craftsmanship, our process actually feels fairly similar. After all, the golden thread in all our works is that we go into detail, nothing stays untouched."

Unlike the exuberantly decorated sets of the old masters' still lifes, Scheltens & Abbenes's are minimal and forgo anything that might be distracting: "The styling props are like pieces of a puzzle that need to be fit," Liesbeth Abbenes notes. "The right props may sometimes provide a solution for a problem, but most of the time, we like to use as few as possible." During the shoots, she often works on the set to arrange the initial composition, while Maurice Scheltens takes care of the camera and lighting. However, in the end everything has to work as a whole, which is why from the preliminary idea to its execution, all creative decisions are made together.

Since every detail counts, the two often find themselves debating about what kind of cropping is right, about how much of an image can be taken away without belittling its impact. They also get all of their postproduction done by the one and only retoucher they trust:

"We have been working with him for many years. He knows exactly to what extent we want our work 'cleaned up.' He also knows about the importance of showing the materials in our work." Most of the time, technical interventions are minimal. "Basically everything one sees has been achieved on set, which we believe supports the integrity of our images. But it also demands a good deal of precision during the process, an attentive back-and-forth between the set and the camera. We have found that preparative sketches don't benefit our process, but rather cause disappointment. Though a significant part of our projects emerges through experimentation, we have to stick our heads together and get all our ideas straight and organized before we begin setting things up."

Scheltens & Abbenes are conceptualists. And, if you will, contextualists—for as much as they seek to develop methods to suit the subject matter, they draw on the particular framework of their commission. Be that an editorial feature or an exhibition, the context always incites them to explore its inherent boundaries. For their ▷

Personal Project for BEOW IN BEELDPRIJS   Photography | Styling   SCHELTENS & ABBENES

Photography

—

Styling

Editorial Project for PIN-UP

SCHELTENS & ABBENES

photo book *Unfolded*, they reversed the conventional hierarchy and chronology of an exhibition and its catalogue: Though initially conceived to document their show at the Jan Cunen museum in Oss (and thus be the last link in the chain), the publication became its blueprint, the beginning of the process. They worked with 3D designers to build small maquettes that resemble the museum building, mounted all the works to be shown on its walls and took pictures of the model to be reproduced in the book. Printed prior to the show, the publication served as a template to set things up, while the show itself was turned into a documentation of its own catalogue.

It was over the course of their making of *Unfolded* that Scheltens & Abbenes discovered how the smartphone could be used as a tool to take photos inside the maquette. "It was amazing what the camera allowed us to see. The snapshots proved a worthwhile step in the process—although in the end, everything had to be worked out in detail." The swiftness of the smartphone snapshot aroused their interest and lead to the potential idea to "study one in depth and reinterpret it, to think a step further and de-familiarize it in order to bring out its randomness."

Anything but random, yet always surprising, Scheltens & Abbenes stand for extraordinary photography that presents products without ever including models. They have heralded a new era of experimentalism in applied still life photography—a genre that is blooming like the opulent bouquets in the works of old painters. While Scheltens & Abbenes attrib-

ute the prosperity of the photographic still life partly to companies who are attempting to cut the production costs of their shoots, they share that part of its success lies in the fact that "many people have discovered that working in that relatively simple way can be pleasantly refreshing." Yet few others master the fine art of the abstract still life with as much flair as Scheltens & Abbenes.

Personal Project

Photography   FRANK STÖCKEL   Art Direction   SASCHA DETTWEILER   Styling   NINA LEMM

Photography   JAN BURWICK   Styling   CHRISTOPH HIMMEL

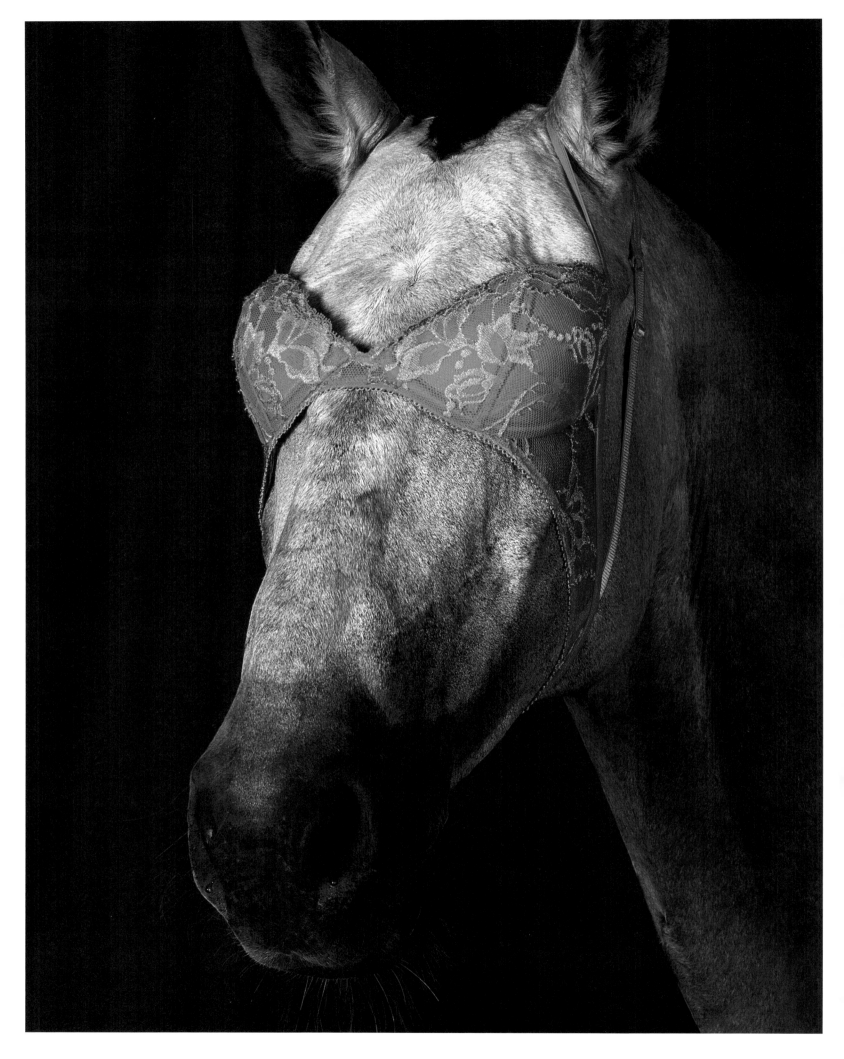

Photography REINHARD HUNGER Styling CHRISTOPH HIMMEL

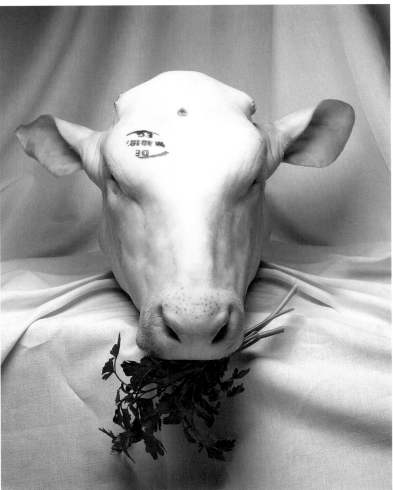

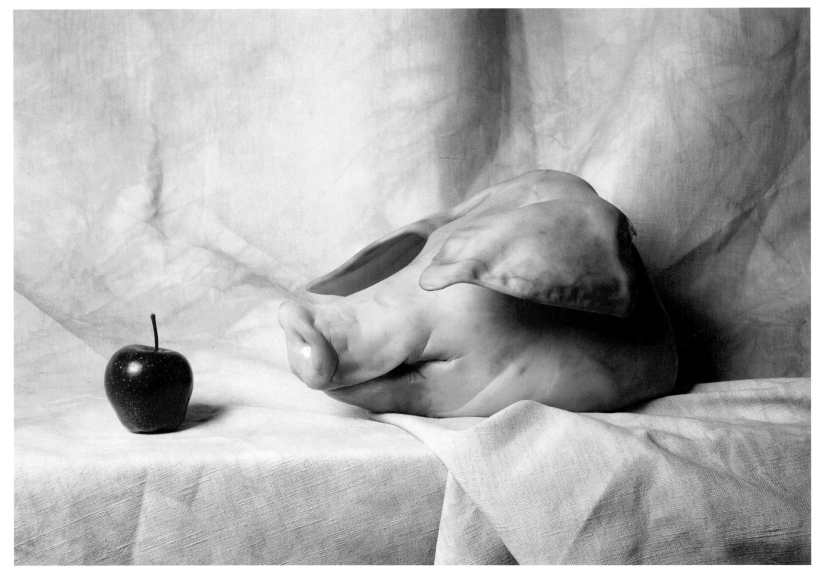

Editorial Project for BEEF!   Photography   REINHARD HUNGER   Styling | Food Styling   VOLKER HOBL

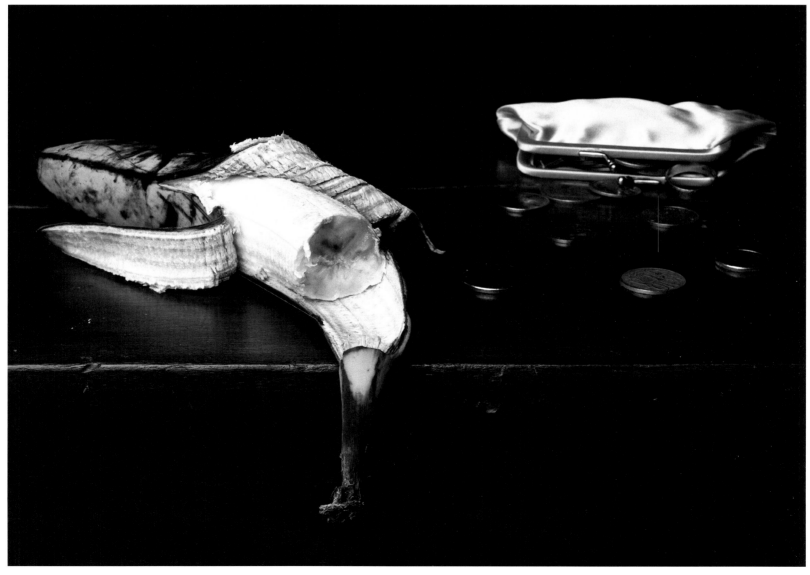

Personal Project   Photography   JUSTINE REYES

Photography OLIVER SCHWARZWALD Styling KIRSTEN SCHMIDT

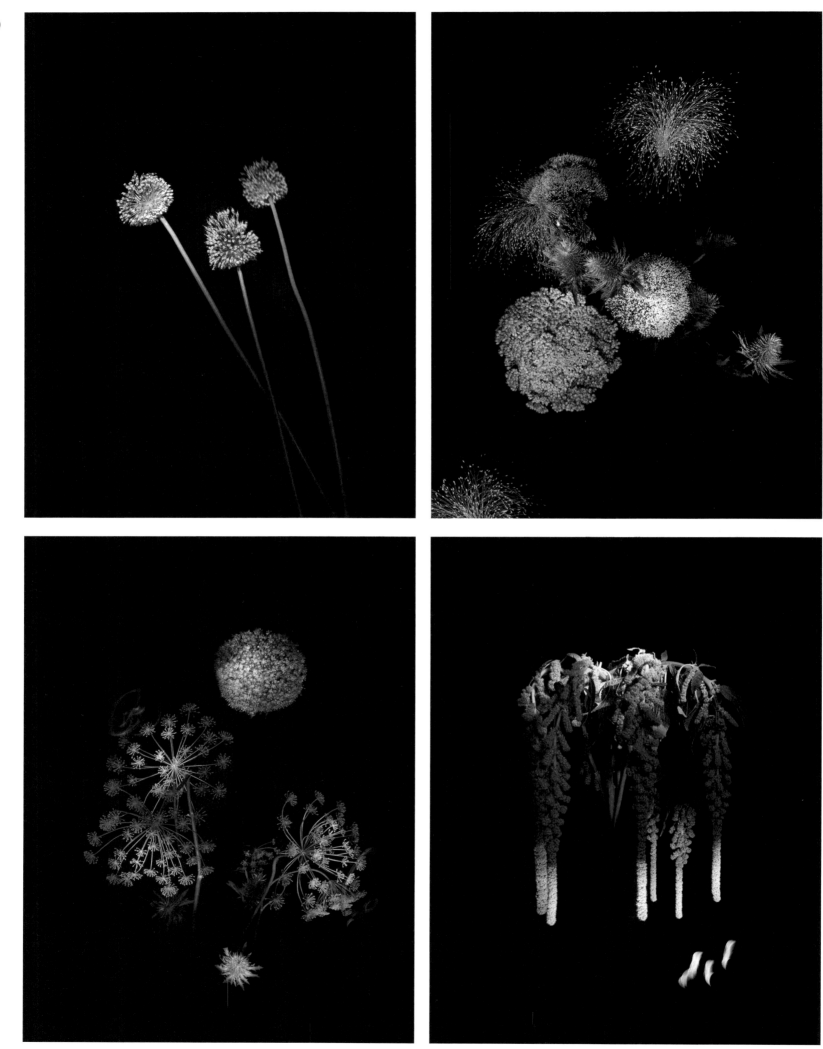

Photography | Styling SARAH ILLENBERGER

Corporate Publishing Project for AUDI MAGAZINE

Photography ATTILA HARTWIG

Styling SARAH ILLENBERGER

Personal Project   Photography | Styling   SARAH ILLENBERGER

Personal Project   Photography   RYAN HOPKINSON   Styling   ANDREW STELLITANO

Art Direction   RYAN HOPKINSON | ANDREW STELLITANO   Matte Painting   ADAM LEARY

Set Design   ANNA BURNS

Photography   MICHAEL BAUMGARTEN

Editorial Project for CASA VOGUE

Personal Project   Photography   STEVE GALLAGHER   Styling   KATIE FORTIS

The chicken, more precisely the partridge, is a classic subject in still life. That is to say it came long before the egg, like the cigarette famously comes after the cake. Most laws of taste are set by tradition. But Milan-based photographer Maurizio Di Iorio likes to lever them out. In his curious stills, eggs are clearly more common than chicken. Some are cracked, others crated in Chanel.

Personal Projects   Photography   <u>MAURIZIO DI IORIO</u>

Inspired by contemporary consumer culture and its unforgiving pace, Di Iorio's photographs feature the stuff that we find squeezed into endless supermarket shelves, crammed into giant shopping malls, or celebrated in the miscellaneous consumption columns of magazines—all the things that commercials are unyieldingly trying to sell us, from toothbrushes to lipsticks. His subjects are not necessarily beautiful, but they are relevant. They are rags of reality, lumps of life, washed up by the tides of insatiable times. ▷

Excited by everything that "expresses our contemporaneity," Di Iorio declares that consumer products and commodities are closely connected to the present, but also to the people who use them. To him, the portrayal of a product parallels that of a person. And while he resolutely rejects the idea of delivering a concrete message through his pictures, he claims that any man-made, lifeless object stands as a symbol of life itself. "A rose isn't simply a beautiful rose," he says. Indeed, it is also a metaphor of mortality when it comes squeezed into a screw clamp. It is in portraying objects that do not merely tell of our time, but also of its transience, that Di Iorio updates the century-old still life concept of vanitas and memento mori.

Much like the old masters who painted their oftentimes mundane objects in organic, meticulous manners, Di Iorio composes his images with immense formal rigor—yet with no penchant for romance.

As can be read on his blog, he "hates landscapes" because they idealize. With words no less sharp than his pictures, Di Iorio leaves no room to doubt that poetic portrayals are none of his business. But whether it be a rose in a screw clamp or a dramatic blaring of spray-on-dew, he overemphasizes thorny details and drop shadows, occasionally to the point where a picture of a product appears more tangible than the actual product itself. To borrow Baudrillard's words, Di Iorio's hyperclear studio stills evoke the notion of a "simulation of something which never really existed." They are imbued with a sense of pulp fiction that turns the trivial into a touchstone of our post-digital faith.

Di Iorio's otherwise organic compositions are all set against solid color backdrops, bright and sober as the seamless studio sweeps. But contrasting the tedious tidiness of conventional commercial shots, his subjects are never perfectly positioned. Instead, they are ▷

MAURIZIO DI IORIO

Photography

Editorial Project for VICE US

Personal Project

Photography

MAURIZIO DI IORIO

Editorial Project for IT'S NICE THAT PRINTED PAGES   Personal Project   Photography   MAURIZIO DI IORIO

broken, nibbled off, crumbled, or a bit out of place. To Di Iorio, perfection is the stepsister of conformity, so he likes to work against it with arrangements that burst with vibrancy and likeable flaws. One could imagine him smashing cans of Campbell's into every picture. Be it out of rebellion—or just because it would look so lusciously red.

Instead of Campbell's, one finds crushed coke cans, nailed nylons, sharply cropped body parts—and certainly a good portion of pastiche and black humor. The most "violent parts of his photographs," however, are their punchy contrasting colors, he reckons. As he sees it, they violate the unwritten rules of so-called good taste, whatever those are worth. Color is, by all means, neither circumstantial nor extraneous in Di Iorio's pictures. It is always equal to form. And although his tints and textures are digitally tuned, he considers his approach "essentially Egglestonian" in nature, noting that despite all the technical tweaks, it is still primarily proper lighting that accounts for crisp colors, like in the good old days of the great William Egglestone.

Much like the legendary street photographer, Di Iorio chooses most of his subjects instinctively: the sight of a product always serves as the initial impulse. From there, he comes to an idea rather rapidly. "The toothbrush photo, perhaps my personal favorite, came together in half an hour, postproduction included. For many pictures the process is longer, but that is mainly due to the time it takes to find the right objects and props. The shooting is so quick because all my compositions have been precisely preconceived." That is where Di Iorio's and Egglestone's paths clearly diverge.

Di Iorio is a dilettante, in the truest sense of the term. Having started photographing for sheer delight, he first pursued the art in parallel to his pre- ▷

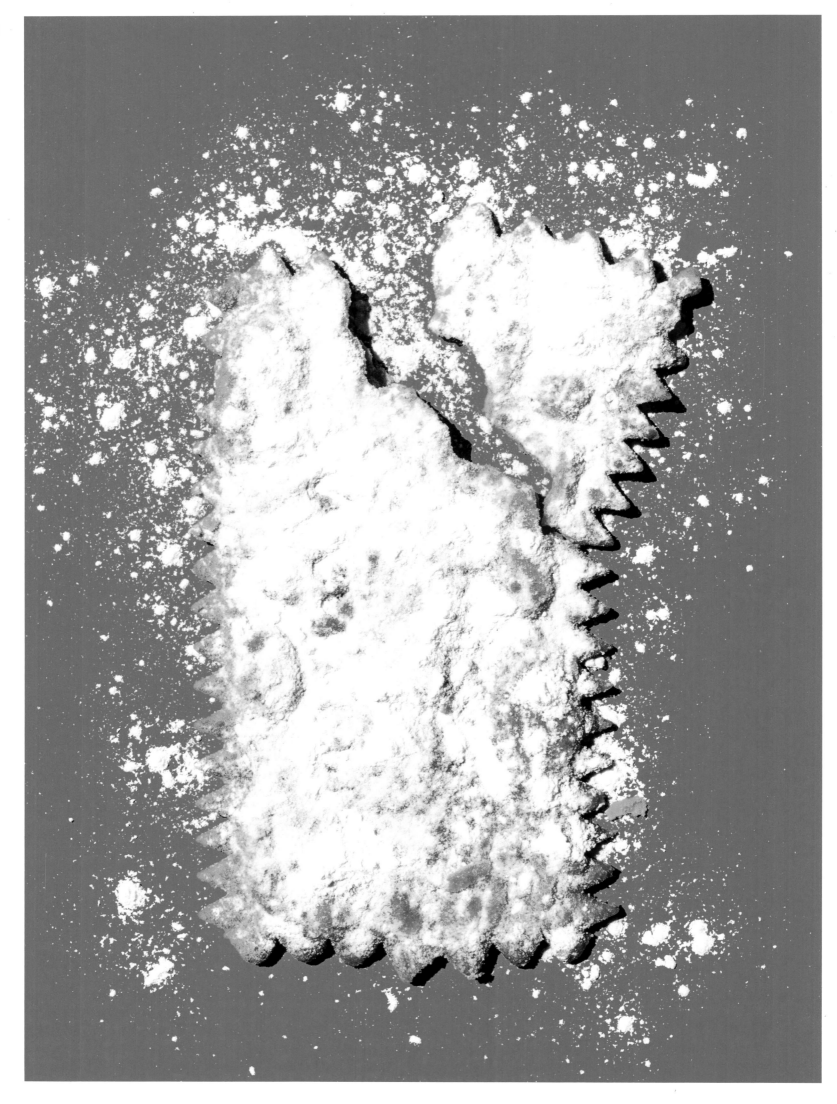

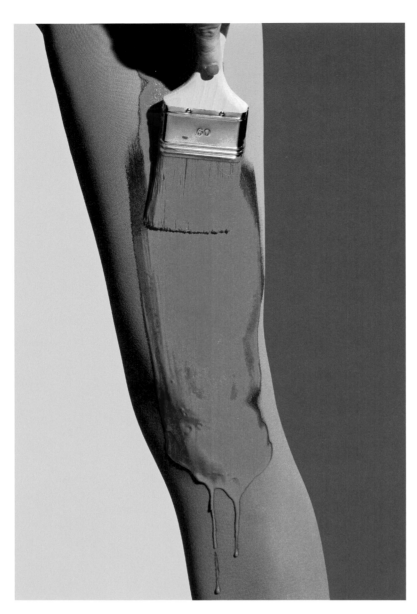

Editorial Project for REFINERY29   Photography   MAURIZIO DI IORIO

vious job as a copywriter in advertising, a career that he opted out of only around four years ago. "I sold words to clients back then, but went home with images in my head," he recounts. Not without reason would he soon counter the common, slightly negative notion of dilettantism with serious commitment. "I started with portraits simply because I didn't have the technical skills to do studio photography back then—but after a while, I found myself devoting entire nights to studying professional studio lighting, because the photography I was fascinated by from the very beginning was the sort that I'm doing now." Namely the carefully composed studio stills that are frequently featured in publications such as *Vogue*, *Vice*, *Wallpaper*, or *Wired*.

Back when he mainly shot portraits, Di Iorio described his process as "a merely predatory act," but that has changed. Everything is entirely in his hands ever since he started shooting stills. "Having full control over the process, it feels a lot like that of a painter working on a picture," he says, bringing us back to the fact that he works with painterly precision. Maniacally attracted by details, Di Iorio has always paid particular attention to technical aspects, which help him bring out fine formal features. He likes to exaggerate and occasionally that culminates in what he calls "a sinister restlessness."

No matter how high-definition, Di Iorio's images spice up the sense of now with a dash of nostalgia. There is something slightly retro to the way they recall clumsily recolored postcards and overdrawn commercials of the past, or more recently of generic, excessively photoshopped early generation stock photos. Perhaps it is precisely in referencing the past that they speak of a collapse of histories that has come to characterize contemporary image culture, and specifically in their careful orchestration that they counter the present's excess of poorly conceived pictures.

"I have nothing against snapshots, but I believe that many photographers abuse the hype to hide their technical flaws," Di Iorio argues, adding that a large part of today's photos will soon be forgotten. Regarding still lifes, he reckons: "For many photographers, especially very young ones, the genre represents nothing but a chance to ▷

Personal Projects   Photography   MAURIZIO DI IORIO

produce simple, often banal, pictures of objects resting against colorful paper backgrounds. No particular attention is given to lighting or composition, and there are rarely any thematic references. A lot of photographs we see on social networks such as Tumblr are flippant images devoid of aesthetic and artistic value. In fact, the number of photographers doing quality still lifes hasn't changed from ten years ago. The rest is just a fad." A fine selection of young photography that Di Iorio does find relevant is featured in the *Disturber*, a publication he has founded to showcase "fearless, in-your-face imagery" by trailblazing talents.

"Photography is a conservative art. Its protagonists have taken years to assimilate the digital. Now, finally, the transition is about to be complete and still life photography gave it the definitive push," declares Di Iorio, for whom "true photographic innovation is in style and in the use of the digital." It is no coincidence his own images strike on both counts. Digitally enhanced and striking in style, they exaggerate the still life's staginess as if to remind us that all products are props, and as such, are replaced at the end of each season. And perhaps to remind us of these poignant words by Guy Debord: "In a world which really is topsy-turvy, the true is a moment of the false."

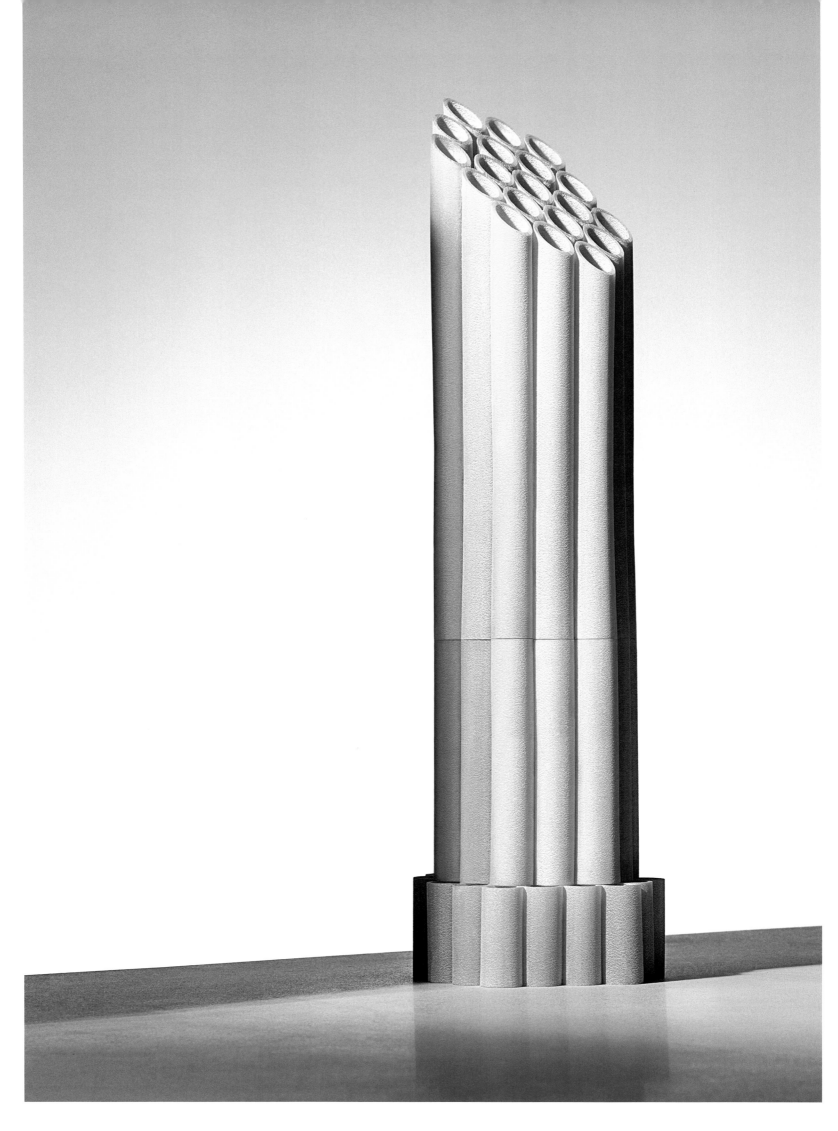

Editorial Project for KINFOLK

Photography   AARON TILLEY   Set Design | Styling   KYLE BEAN   Food Styling   IAIN GRAHAM

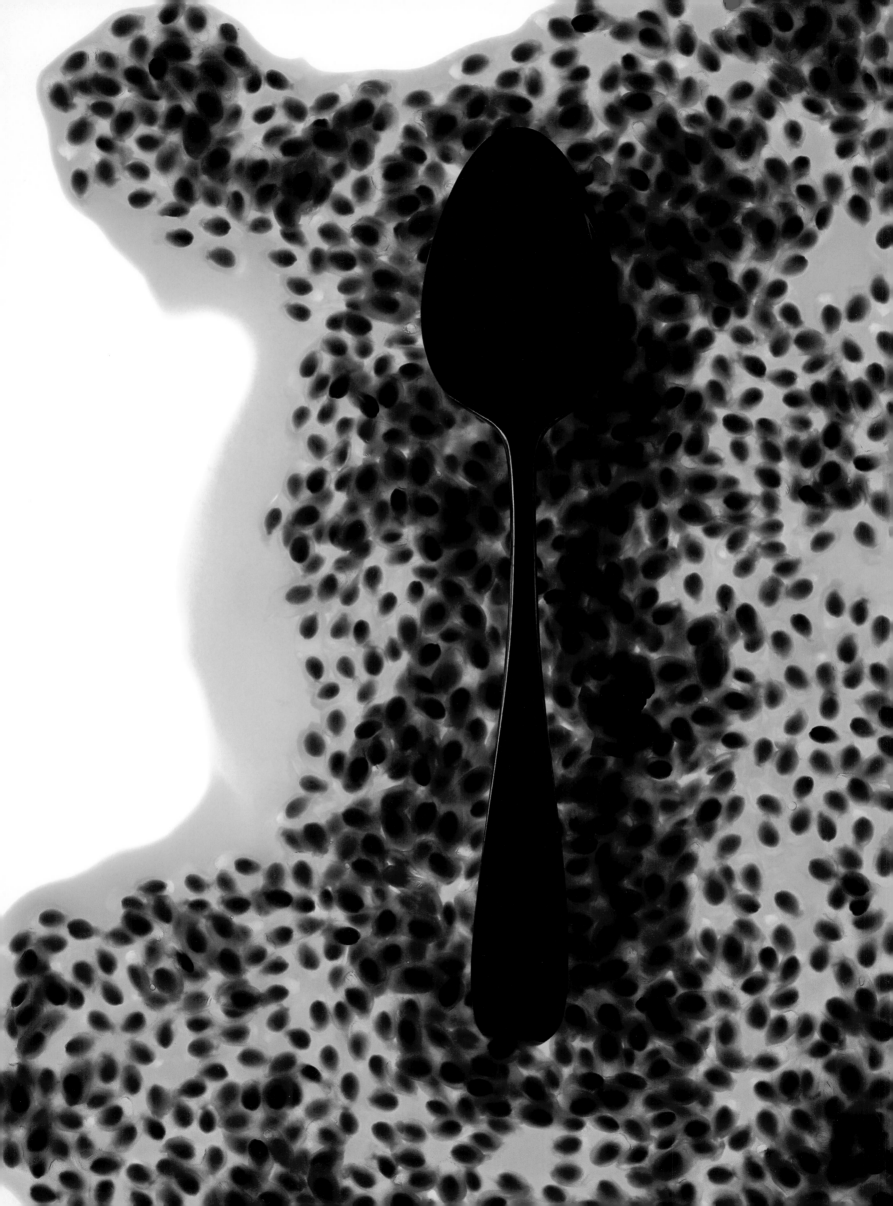

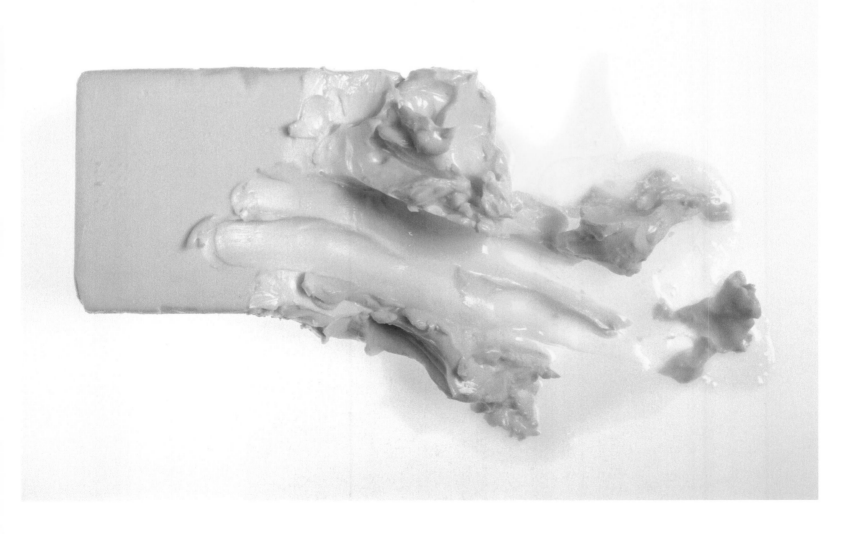

Editorial Project for THE GOURMAND   Photography   GUSTAV ALMESTAL   Food Styling   NIKLAS HANSEN

Corporate Project for KINTUGI   Photography   SAM HOFMAN   Styling   ANDREW STELLITANO

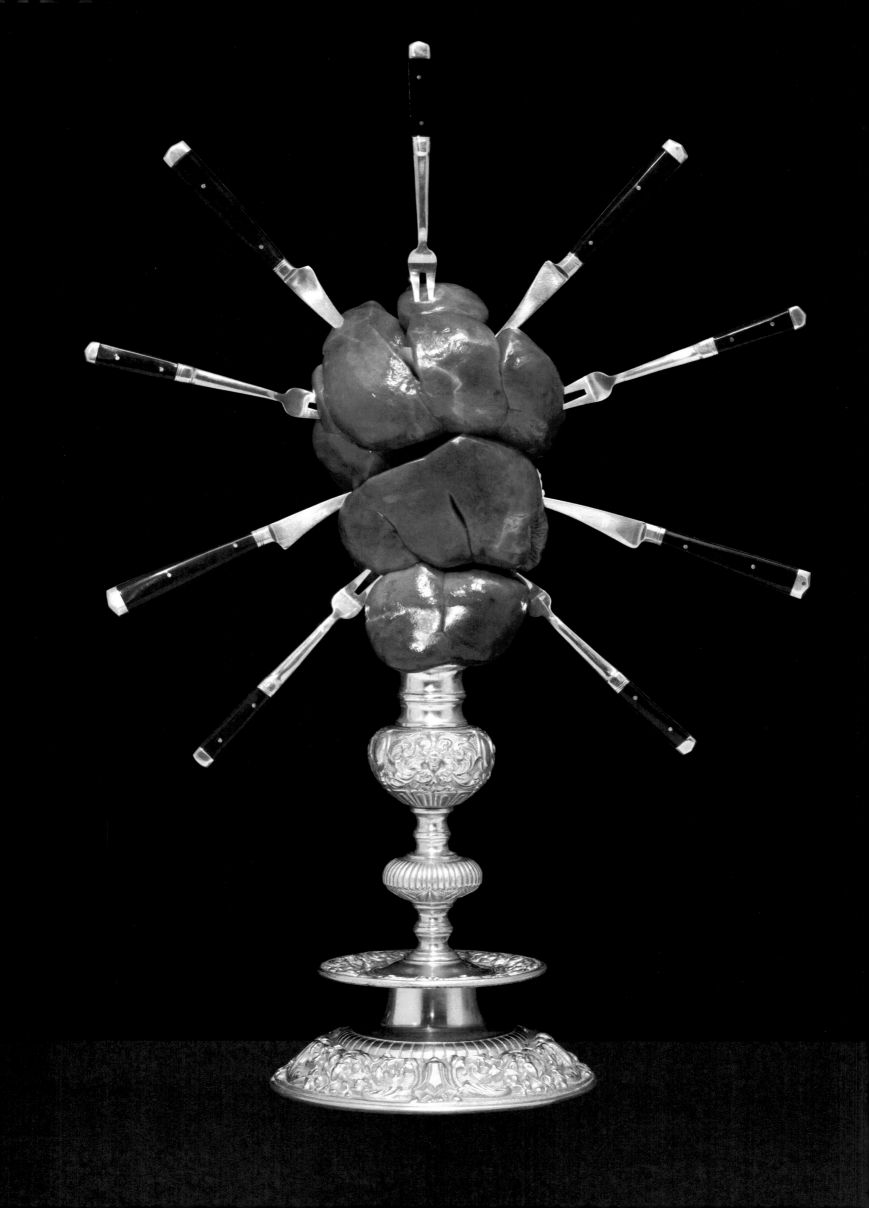

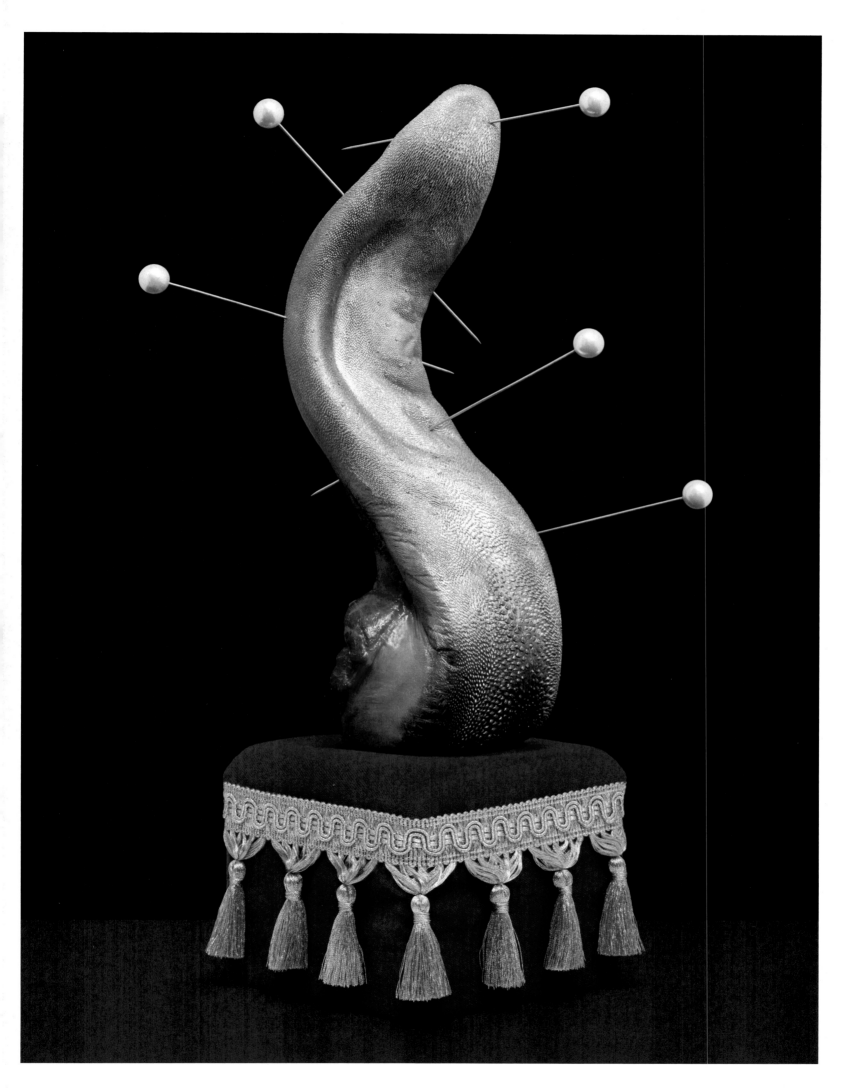

Editorial Project for SWALLOW MAGAZINE

Photography   BELA BORSODI   Prop Styling   JOJO LI   Food Styling   VICTORIA GRANOF

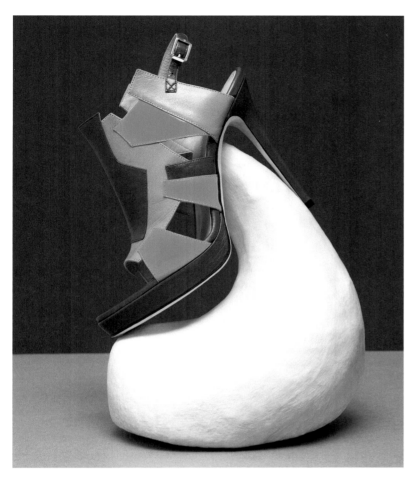

Editorial Project for FRÄULEIN

Photography   BELA BORSODI   Prop Styling   JOJO LI   Fashion Styling   VANESSA GIUDICI

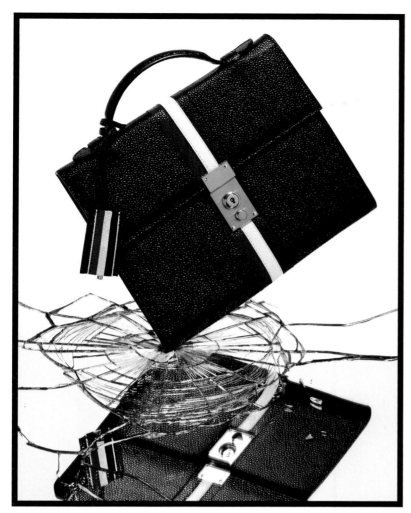

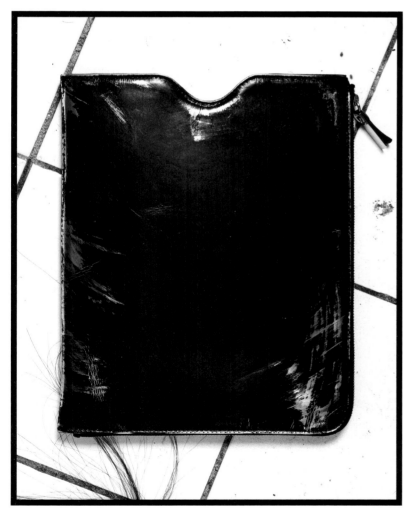

Editorial Project for L'OFFICIEL HOMME   Photography   BELA BORSODI

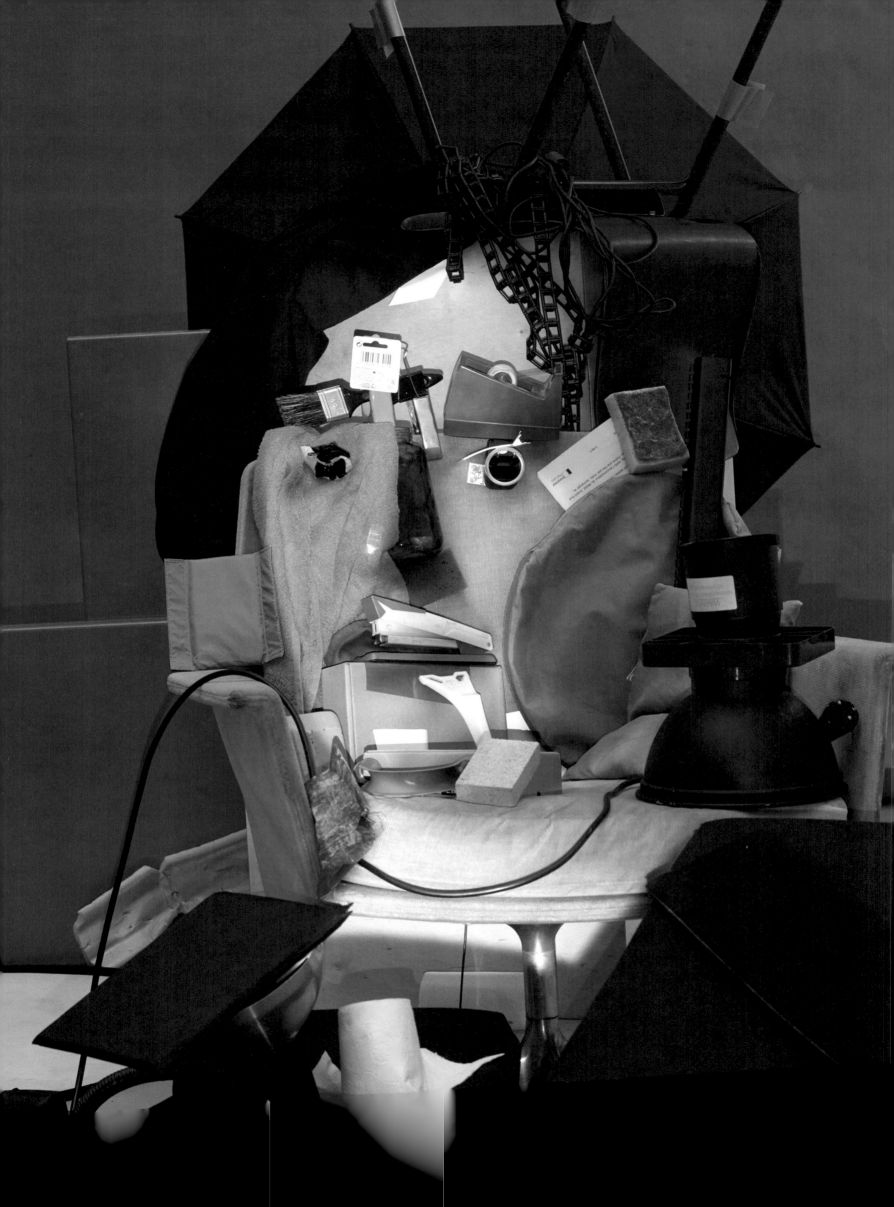

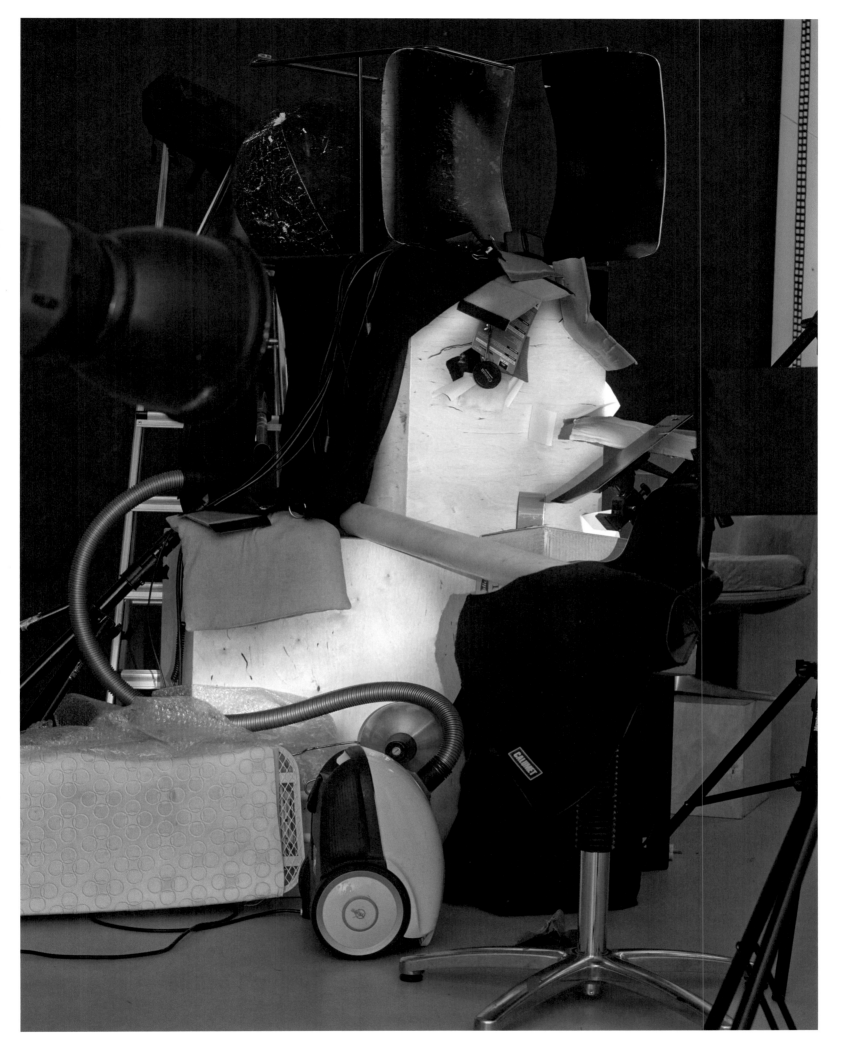

Corporate Project for MERKELBACH   Photography   BLOMMERS SCHUMM

FEATURE: <u>PETER LANGER</u>

From Adidas Superstar sneakers to Zuhair Murad glamorous gowns, iconic fashion items have always spoken a language of their own. Ever since the German *ZEITmagazin* started publishing a popular weekly style column featuring striking full-page still life photographs captured by Peter Langer, fashion began to speak Langer's language, who in fact lets garments speak for themselves through the fall of their folds and fine fabrics. And we listen. Or, rather, look at Langer's pictures with a hint of longing. Less for the luxury they exude than for the life of their own they seem to take.

Occasionally, Langer's images speak of the frenzy of the fashion world, but above all, they speak to us in an utterly intimate way, reminding us of our own relationship with what we wear. By arranging clothes in innovative combinations and against unforeseen backdrops, Langer creates visual contrasts that produce very subjective stories. He lets us read between the lines of Burberry checks and pinstripe suits or into the flowing forms of the garments.

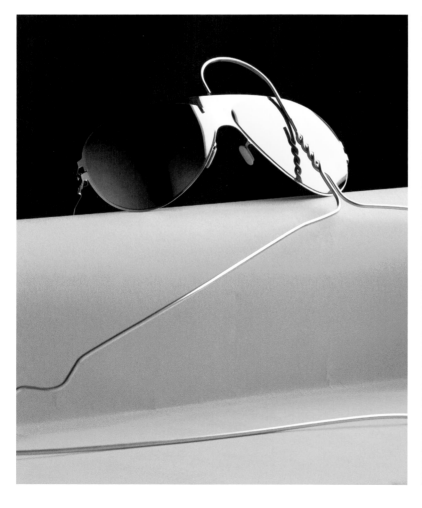

Editorial Project for ZEITMAGAZIN

| Photography | Concept | Styling | Set Design | PETER LANGER |

Set Design | Concept | Photography

Editorial Project for **M LE MAGAZINE DU MONDE**

"It is not easy to take a good photograph," Langer says, and by good photograph he means one that makes a meaningful point. "Without a story, you have dead images, which are merely two-dimensional copies of reality. If you want to create something new, you need some sort of narrative; you need to construct tension by choosing the suitable ingredients and blending them in a surprising way. It's a bit like cook-

ing." Indeed, Langer's compositions contain a sweet sense of storytelling, spiced up with a hint of humor and humanity.

Presenting inanimate products in unexpected arrangements, Langer's photographs have us reeling between composition and chaos, romanticism and mayhem, familiarity and otherness. Ironically, it is in removing themselves from the conventional image buildup that these photographs bring the products ▷

CHANEL

they feature closer to us. Where other fashion stills feel indifferent, Langer's connect with us on an astoundingly personal level, countering flat lay shots with suggestive structures and thwarting the traditional still life with lively compositions and dynamic drapes.

Speaking of movement: Automobiles are a recurrent motif in Langer's work. From the weirdly cropped Porsche displayed in a car dealer's window that Langer posted on his prolific photo blog back in 1999 to the truck tarpaulins presenting a blown-up luxury bag by Lanvin, they return, like partridges in the paintings of Flemish masters, as if to reproduce a mechanical slice of modern life. Shoes also appear as a pattern in Langer's work. They are arguably the most fetishized fashion item of all, and Langer considers them "perfect models" that "simply always look good."

His pictures deal with beauty, he says, but it does not seem to be the kind of beauty that strives for perfection. Rather, it is a type of beauty that lies in the essence of things, in their odd fragments that one every so often fails to recognize. Like the wise thinkers Plato, Aristotle, and later Leibniz, Langer does not dedicate himself to the object in toto, but focuses on the set of attributes that seem integral to its identity, and thus likes to zoom in on things to combine close ups with sectional views of structures. "A core element of still life photography deals with surfaces and the nature of material," he notes, "so being close to the object is one of the best tools to enhance and fetishize it."

Before starting his career as a photographer, Peter Langer worked as an art director in advertising. On the one hand, he appears to cite commercial photography in his appropria-

tion of certain advertising aesthetics through pictures that are attractive, seductive, and suggestive. On the other hand, Langer thwarts this aesthetic genre by pulling haute fashion down from its high horse and placing it side by side with simple, everyday objects. Desire in Langer's photographs either recedes into the background or is ironically exaggerated by overly allusive backdrops.

Langer's images feature the latest fashion items, but deserve to be called dernier cri themselves. Aside from the acclaimed weekly style page in *ZEITmagazin*, his photographs appear in *M Le Magazine du Monde* and other renowned publications on a regular basis. Thematically, and technically too, they are multi-layered and, like the photograph of a Louis Vuitton trolley that is blatantly juxtaposed on top of lush meadows, montaged in unexpected ways. Accordingly, image processing represents an integral part of Langer's process, much more than a mere touch-up phase to apply filters on formal features. As he puts it, it has "really emancipated from its 'post' role to become a part that is actually as ▷

Editorial Project for ZEITMAGAZIN   Photography | Concept | Styling   PETER LANGER

Editorial Project for FAZ MAGAZIN   Photography   PETER LANGER   Styling   WINNIE PLACZKO

Editorial Projects for ZEITMAGAZIN

Photography | Concept | Styling | Set Design | PETER LANGER

tant as the image-making itself, sometimes even superior to the shooting. One might say it relates back to the original meaning of the term 'photographic.' In fact, I feel more graphic than photo. I like to shift little squares, trying to solve a backlit puzzle. I am also not hidden in a dark room, everything happens in bright light."

Imagine Langer in a brashly lit studio. This is an image that aptly leads to the observation that his own are occasionally overexposed, as if glared by halogen headlights: It supports their strong sense of immediacy and highlights

the notion that they are no less suggestive than the smartphone snapshots that have come to dominate contemporary image culture. Langer remarks that "in the western world, the iPhone picture has long won over the studio shot, taken with a pricey professional camera," and refers to Apple's recent ad campaign constituting a series of photos "shot with an iPhone 6." In the age of Instagram and Facebook, "form has long lost its privileged position to content." And Peter Langer likes this.

He himself mixes "expensive" and "cheap" imagery, as he ▷

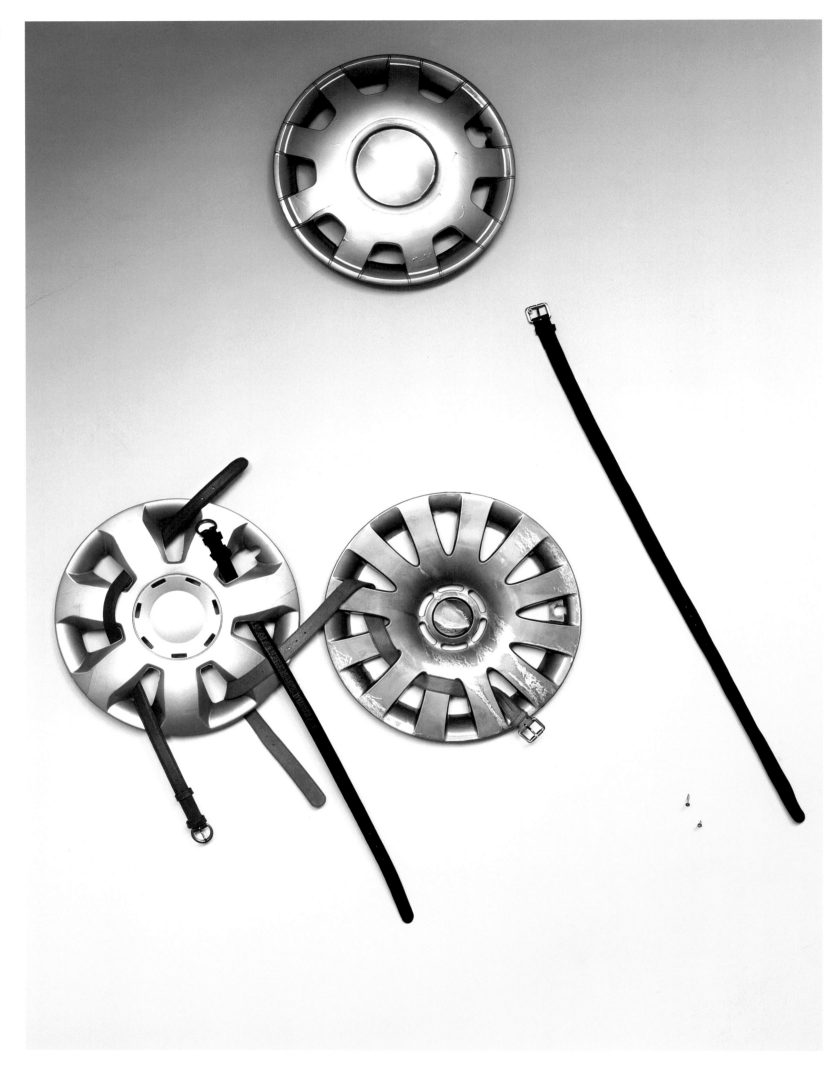

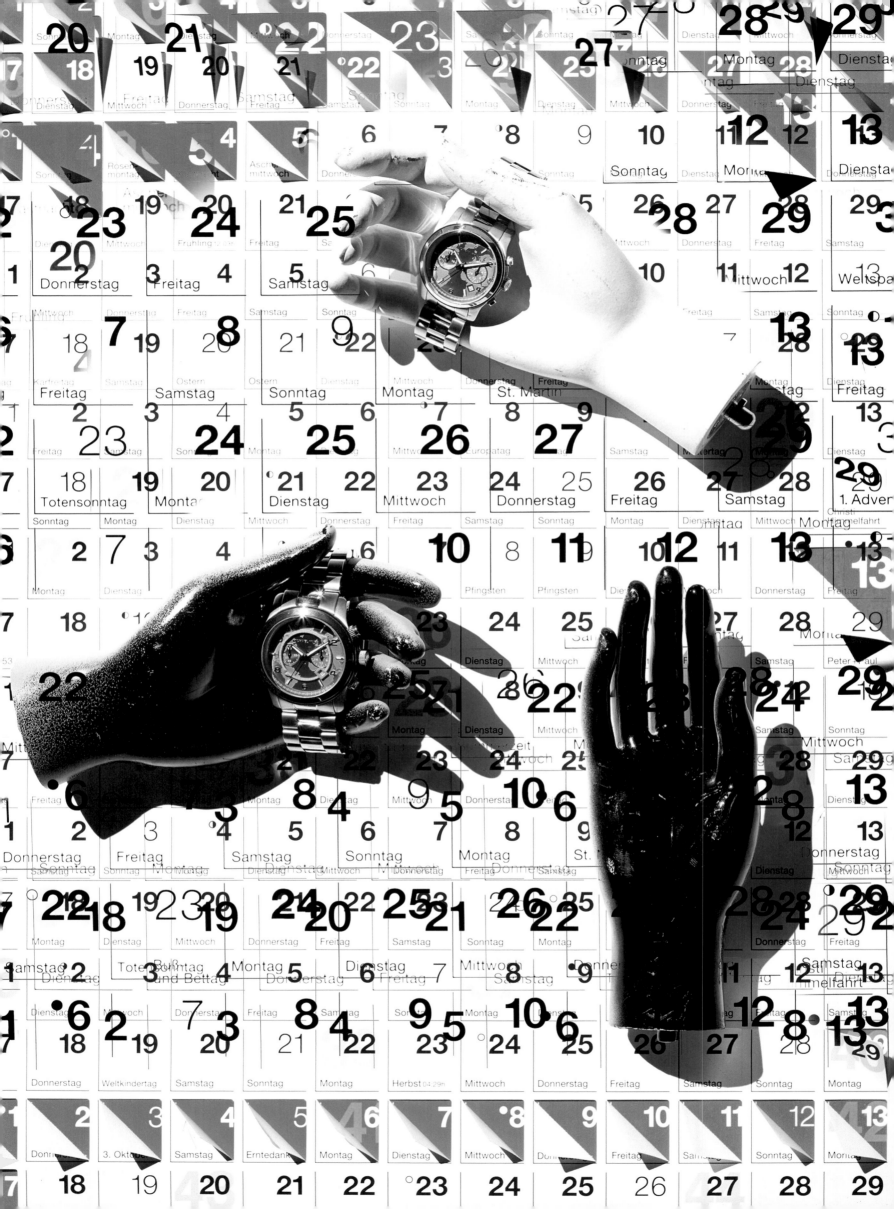

Editorial Project for ZEITMAGAZIN

Photography | Concept | Styling | Set Design | PETER LANGER

calls it, in combining photos from his iPhone with high-end studio shots bolstered by the latest digital technologies. "Nowadays there is no black or white," he affirms. "We live in a time when there is a lot of gray-scaling. I think this is very liberating and I am glad to work under these circumstances." Image hierarchies feel flat in an age when visual content is copied and pasted, compressed, reproduced, reformatted, reedited, remixed, and oftentimes distributed for free in the form of rags and rips that swiftly pass our digital pipelines. Langer's pictures are deeply ingrained in that time, and much like his approach to image making, their compositions present themselves as pleasantly democratic.

Precious gowns and gas pumps, swimming pools and silver pumps, leather coats and car logos, toy dinosaurs and deluxe trainers. All of these things are on par in Langer's pictures. And oftentimes, as we know it from fashion, the most clashing combinations make for the best matches. Any supposed break in style encourages many possible interpretations. It is in this in-between space of seemingly ill-suited haute couture and low(er) profile products that Langer's stories begin.

While the actual product is always predetermined by the client, Langer adds other objects to the composition until it clicks. "It is largely work in progress, starting with a little idea, and ending up somewhere totally different," Langer says. "To compose a masterpiece, one must assume, but at the same time relinquish control while shooting, and accept that to some extent, it's really a trial and error process. In fact, the hardest part is to know when to stop and call it a final image." It is about staying alert in what he calls an "ongoing struggle between order and chaos," which sounds like the challenge of life itself.

In Langer's opinion, the chaotic circumstances of our contemporary world contribute to the recent success of the still life. One of the reasons why this particular genre of photography is receiving such great attention lately is, according to Langer, because of our growing longing for control and security, that is itself a reaction to all the visual and verbal information that has been inundating the world since the early days of the digital revolution. "We are all longing for guidance, looking for clarity and some sort of overall order. People want to be put in place and put things in place themselves." Which relates back to still life photography. "Its easier without people."

Editorial Project for ZEITMAGAZIN

Photography | Concept | Set Design | PETER LANGER | Styling | ANETT STEINBRECHER

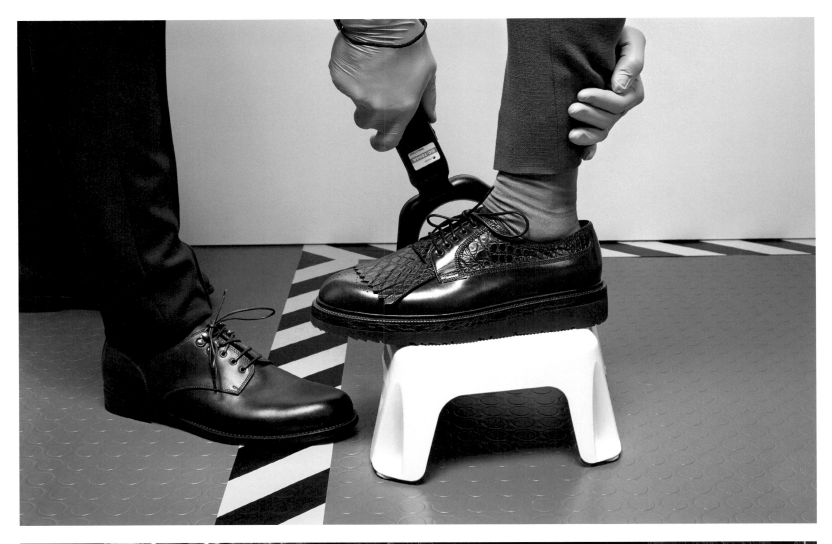

Editorial Project for M LE MAGAZINE DU MONDE

Photography | Concept MIRKA LAURA SEVERA Styling LILLY MARTHE EBENER

INDEX

P. 4-5
Photography JENNY VAN SOMMERS
www.jennyvansommers.com
Set Design RACHEL THOMAS
www.rachelthomasstudio.com

P. 6-9
Photography, Styling LISELOTTE WATKINS
c/o LundLund

P. 10-11
Photography JENNY VAN SOMMERS
www.jennyvansommers.com
Set Design RACHEL THOMAS
www.rachelthomasstudio.com

P. 12-13
Photography BELA BORSODI
www.belaborsodi.com
Styling RHIANNA RULE
www.rhiannarulestyling.tumbler.com

P. 14-15
Photography, Art Direction, Styling
MARCELO KRASILCIC
www.mercelok.com

P. 16
Photography, Art Direction
MARCELO KRASILCIC
www.mercelok.com
Styling BENEDETTA DELL'ORTO
www.benedettadellorto.com

P. 17-19
Photography, Art Direction, Styling
MARCELO KRASILCIC
www.mercelok.com

P. 20-21
Photography, Art Direction JESS BONHAM
www.jessbonham.co.uk
Styling, Art Direction ANNA LOMAX
www.annalomax.com

P. 22-23
Photography, Art Direction, Styling AKATRE
www.akatre.com

P. 24-25
Photography, Art Direction, Styling PUTPUT
www.putput.dk

P. 26-27
Photography, Set Design QIU YANG
www.qiu-yang.com
Set Design MICHAEL SCHONER
www.michaelschoner.de

P. 28-29
Photography QIU YANG
www.qiu-yang.com
Set Design ELENA MORA
www.elenamora.com

P. 30-31
Photography, Set Design QIU YANG
www.qiu-yang.com
Set Design, Styling SARAH-JANE HOFFMANN
www.sarahjanehoffmann.com
Fashion Styling THE BALLROOM

P. 32-33
Photography, Set Design QIU YANG
www.qiu-yang.com
Set Design SARAH-JANE HOFFMANN
www.sarahjanehoffmann.com

P. 34
Photography, Styling, Set Design
STILLS & STROKES
www.stillsandstrokes.com

P. 35
Photography, Styling, Set Design
STILLS & STROKES
www.stillsandstrokes.com
Concept FINJA ROSENTHAL
www.rosenthal.de
Magazine Art Direction MARIO LOMBARDO
www.mariolombardo.com
Smoothies STUDIOBUS

P. 36
Photography, Styling, Set Design
STILLS & STROKES
www.stillsandstrokes.com
Art Direction MARIO LOMBARDO
www.mariolombardo.com

P. 37
Photography, Styling, Set Design
STILLS & STROKES
www.stillsandstrokes.com
Magazine Art Direction MIKE MEIRÉ
www.meireundmeire.de
Magazine Fashion Styling ANDREA PORRO
www.gq.com

P. 38-43
Photography, Styling, Set Design
STILLS & STROKES
www.stillsandstrokes.com
Magazine Art Direction MIKE MEIRÉ
www.meireundmeire.de

P. 44-45
Photography, Styling, Set Design
STILLS & STROKES
www.stillsandstrokes.com
Magazine Art Direction MIKE MEIRÉ
www.meireundmeire.de
Magazine Art Direction MELISSA SIMPEMBA
www.garagemag.com

P. 46-47
Photography, Styling, Set Design
STILLS & STROKES
www.stillsandstrokes.com
Magazine Art Direction MIKE MEIRÉ
www.meireundmeire.de

P. 48-49
Photography, Styling, Set Design
STILLS & STROKES
www.stillsandstrokes.com
Magazine Art Direction MIRKO BORSCHE
www.mirkoborsche.com

P. 50-51
Photography VINCENT GAPAILLARD
www.vincentgapaillard.com
Styling LILLY MARTHE EBENER
www.lillymarthe-ebener.com
Set Design MARILYN PERROD & JONATHAN BEY
www.maylinperrod.wordpress.com
www.jonathanbey.com
Magazine Art Direction
CHRISTIAN RAVERA & GUY GUGLIERI
www.mixte.com

P. 52-53
Photography, Art Direction, Styling
CHARLES NEGRE
www.charlesnegre.com

P. 54-57
Photography, Art Direction, Styling
PHILIPPE FRAGNIERE
www.philippefragniere.ch

P. 58-59
Photography KATE JACKLING
www.katejackling.com
Styling LEILA LATCHIN
www.leilalatchin.com

P. 60-61
Photography THOMAS BROWN
www.thomasbrown.info
Styling DAVID WHITE
www.davidwhitesetdesign.com

P. 62-63
Photography, Set Design
CARL KLEINER
www.carlkleiner.com

P. 64-65
Photography, Art Direction, Styling
CHRISTIAN HAGEMANN
www.christian-hagemann.com

P. 66-67
Photography THOMAS BROWN
www.thomasbrown.info
Art Direction ROBERT STOREY
www.storeystudio.com

P. 68-69
Photography DAN TOBIN SMITH
www.dantobinsmith.com
Magazine Creative Direction
GRAHAM ROUNTHWAITE
www.i-d.vice.com

P. 70-71
Photography THOMAS DE MONACO
www.thomasdemonaco.com
Magazine Art Direction
JEAN DENIS MONÉGIER DU SORBIER
www.sochicmagazine.com

P. 72
Photography, Art Direction, Styling
KENJI AOKI
www.aokiphoto.com

P. 73
Photography, Styling KENJI AOKI
www.aokiphoto.com
Magazine Art Direction
ABBEY KUSTER-PROKELL
www.realsimple.com

P. 74-75
Photography PAUL LEPREUX
www.paullepreux.com
Art Direction, Set Design
ROMAIN LENANCKER
www.lenancker.com

P. 76-77
Photography JAN BURWICK
www.janburwick.de
c/o Wildfox Running
Styling CHRISTOPH HIMMEL
www.christophhimmel.de
c/o Liganord

P. 78-79
Photography MICHAEL BAUMGARTEN
www.michaelbaumgarten.com

P. 80-81
Photography MICHAEL BODIAM
www.michaelbodiam.com
Styling, Set Design SARAH PARKER
www.sarahparkercreative.com
Magazine Art Direction
HAAKON SPENCER & MATTHEW FENTON
www.ma-ad.ch/verities

P. 82-83
Photography MICHAEL BAUMGARTEN
www.michaelbaumgarten.com
Magazine Art Direction, Styling
CHRISTIANE JUERGENSEN
www.celine.com

P. 84-85
Photography, Art Direction, Set Design
BENOIT PAILLEY
www.benoitpailley.com
Styling INES FENDRI
www.inesfendri.tumbler.com

P. 86-87
Photography, Styling BOHMAN+SJÖSTRAND
www.bohmansjostrand.com
Art Direction EBBA BLOMGREN
www.cattochco.se
Styling LOTTA AGATON
www.lottaagaton.se

P. 88-91
Photography BLOMMERS SCHUMM
www.blommers-schumm.com

P. 92-93
Photography, Art Directiom LENA C.EMERY
www.lenaemery.com
Styling RAQUEL GARCIA

P. 94
Photography MICHAEL BODIAM
www.michaelbodiam.com
Styling, Set Design SARAH PARKER
www.sarahparkercreative.com
Magazine Art Direction SAM WALTON
www.slwcreative.com

P. 95
Photography THOMAS POPINGER
c/o Stillstars www.stillstars.de

P. 96-97
Photography JOSS MCKINLEY
www.jossmckinley.com
Styling YANN LECORCHE
www.lecorche.com
Floral Design PIERRE BANCHEREAU
www.debeaulieu-paris.com

P. 98-99
Photography PAUL LEPREUX
www.paullepreux.com
Styling, Magazine Fashion Editing
KATHRIN SEIDEL
www.elle.de

P. 100-101
Photography VINCENT GAPAILLARD
www.vincentgapaillard.com
Styling MAYA ZEPINIC
www.mayazepinic.tumbler.com
Set Design MARCEL VAN DOORN
www.marcelvandoorn.com

Magazine Art Direction JAMIE PERLMAN
www.vogue.co.uk

P. 102-103
Photography THOMAS DE MONACO
www.thomasdemonaco.com
Magazine Fashion Direction LISA TUCKER
www.frenchrevue.com

P. 104-105
Photography VINCENT GAPAILLARD
www.vincentgapaillard.com
Styling HERMIONE HARBAS
www.hermioneharbas.com
Set Design RONAN TEISSÈDRE
Magazine Art Direction GIORGIO MARTINOLI
www.airfrance.com

P. 106-109
Photography, Art Direction, Styling
CHARLES NEGRE
www.charlesnegre.com

P. 110-111
Photography HAW-LIN SERVICES
www.haw-lin-services.com
Magazine Art Direction ELIZIA DI FONZO

P. 112-113
Photography LEANDRO FARINA
www.leandrofarina.com
Styling ANNETTE MASTERMAN
www.annettemasterman.com

P.114-115
Photography PAUL LEPREUX
www.paullepreux.com
ArtDirection, Set Design ROMAIN LENANCKER
www.lenancker.com

P.116-117
Photography, Art Direction, Styling
CHARLES NEGRE
www.charlesnegre.com

P.118-119
Photography AARON TILLEY
www.aarontilley.com
Art Direction SANDY MACLENNAN
www.eastcentralstudios.com

P.120-123
Photography BLOMMERS SCHUMM
www.blommers-schumm.com

P.124-126
Photography, Art Direction JESS BONHAM
www.jessbonham.co.uk
Styling, Art Direction ANNA LOMAX
www.annalomax.com

P.126-129
Photography METZ+RACINE
www.metzracine.com
Set Design HERVÉ SAUVAGE
www.hervesauvage.com
Magazine Art Direction and Styling
LAURENCE HOVART
www.numero.com

P.130-131
Photography, Art Direction METZ+RACINE
www.metzracine.com
Set Design, Furniture Styling HERVÉ SAUVAGE
www.hervesauvage.com
Fashion Styling STORNY+MISERICORDIA
www.stornymisericordia.com

P.132-133
Photography, Art Direction METZ+RACINE
www.metzracine.com
Art Direction, Research ARABESCHI DI LATTE
www.arabeschidilatte.org
Food Styling FRANCESCA SARTI

P.134-135
Photography METZ+RACINE
www.metzracine.com
Art Direction, Set Design ROMAIN LENANCKER
www.lenancker.com
Magazine Art Direction ARMIN MORBACH
www.tushmagazine.com

P.136-137
Photography, Art Direction METZ+RACINE
www.metzracine.com
Set Design, Furniture Styling JANINA PEDAN
www.pedan.co.uk
Fashion Styling MADELEINE ØSTLIE
www.madelaineostlie.com

P. 138-139
Photography METZ+RACINE
www.metzracine.com
Styling JANE HOWARD
www.archivist.cc
Set Design DAVID WHITE
www.davidwhitesetdesign.com

P. 140-141
Photography METZ+RACINE
www.metzracine.com
Set Design JANINA PEDAN
www.pedan.co.uk
Magazine Art Direction ROCKWELL HARWOOD
www.details.com

P.142-143
Photography, Art Direction METZ+RACINE
www.metzracine.com
Styling CLÉMENCE CAHU
www.clemencecahu.com
Set Design GEORGINA PRAGNELL
www.georginapragnell.com

P.144-145
Photography JOSS MCKINLEY
www.jossmckinley.com
Magazine Jewelry Editing, Styling
VICTORIA BAIN
www.victoria-bain.com

P. 146-147
Photography CHRISTOFFER DARKALS
www.darkals.se

P. 148-149
Photography CHRISTIAN HAGEMANN
www.christian-hagemann.com
Magazine Art Direction YVES GERTEIS
Magazine Fashion Direction RICHARD WIDMER
www.sistyle.ch

P. 150-151
Photography, Art Direction BAKER&EVANS
www.bbde.co.uk
Magazine Art Direction SEETAL SOLANKI
www.seetalsolanki.com
Styling SARAH PARKER
www.sarahparkercreative.com

P. 152-153
Photography JOSS MCKINLEY
www.jossmckinley.com
Styling LEILA LATCHIN
www.leilalatchin.com

P. 154-155
Photography OLIVER SCHWARZWALD
www.oliverschwarzwald.de
Styling ELENA MORA
www.elenamora.com

P. 156-157
Photography SAM HOFMAN
www.samhofman.co.uk
Styling KYLE BEAN
www.kylebean.co.uk

P. 158-159
Photography, Set Design BENOIT PAILLEY
www.benoitpailley.com
Magazine Art Direction ERIC PILLAULT
Magazine Fashion Editing, Styling
FIONA KHALIFA
www.lemonde.fr

P. 160-161
Photography, Styling KENJI AOKI
www.aokiphoto.com
Magazine Art Direction
ABBEY KUSTER-PROKELL
www.realsimple.com

P. 162-163
Photography BOHMAN+SJÖSTRAND
www.bohmansjostrand.com
Art Direction PETER HERRMANN
www.garbergsproject.se

P. 164-165
Photography, Art Direction, Styling AKATRE
www.akatre.com

P. 166-167
Photography HAW-LIN SERVICES
www.haw-lin-services.com
Postproduction RGBERLIN
www.rgberlin.com

P. 168-169
Photography ATTILA HARTWIG
www.attilahartwig.com
Styling NINA LEMM
www.ninalemm.com c/o Liganord
Assistant DAVID DÖRRAST

P. 170-171
Photography KLAUS ALTEVOGT
www.altevogt-fotografie.de
Styling ANKE LACHMUTH
c/o Liganord

P. 172-173
Photography, Concept, Set Design
MIRKA LAURA SEVERA
www.severafrahm.com
Magazine Art Direction ERIC PILLAULT
www.lemonde.fr
Styling ALINE DE BEAUCLAIRE
www.alinedebeauclaire.com
Postproduction MICHAEL FRAHM
www.severafrahm.com

P. 174-175
Photography LUKE KIRWAN
www.lukekirwan.com
Magazine Art Direction LARA FERROS
www.elleuk.com

P. 176-177
Photography BAKER & EVANS
www.bbde.co.uk
Brand Art Direction COS
www.cosstores.com

Styling SARAH PARKER
www.sarahparkercreative.com

P. 178-179
Photography, Set Design CARL KLEINER
www.carlkleiner.com
Art Direction EVERETT PELAYO
www.everettpelayo.com

P. 180-181
Photography, Art Direction, Set Design
MIRKA LAURA SEVERA
www.severafrahm.com
Postproduction MICHAEL FRAHM
www.severafrahm.com

P. 182-183
Photography BOHMAN+SJÖSTRAND
www.bohmansjostrand.com
Art Direction MAJA KÖLQVIST
www.kolqvist.se

P. 184-185
Photography KATE JACKLING
www.katejackling.com
Jewelry LINDA BROTHWELL
www.lindabrothwell.com

P. 186-187
Photography, Art Direction, Set Design
GIULIA MUNARI
www.munstudio.co
Styling, Jewelry JORINDE MELINE BARKE
www.jmb-jewelry.com

P. 188-189
Photography, Art Direction, Styling
CHARLES NEGRE
www.charlesnegre.com
Jewelry ETIENNE GARACHON

P. 190-191
Photography CARL KLEINER
www.carlkleiner.com
Set Design AGATA BELECEN
www.agatabelecen.com
Postproduction JOSEPH COLLEY

P. 192-195
Photography, Styling SCHELTENS & ABBENES
www.scheltens-abbenes.com
Art Direction OLIVIER SAILLARD
www.palaisgalliera.paris.fr

P. 196-197
Photography, Styling SCHELTENS & ABBENES
www.scheltens-abbenes.com

P. 198-199
Photography, Styling SCHELTENS & ABBENES
Magazine Art Direction
JOP VAN BENNEKOM, GERT JONKERS
www.thegentlewoman.co.uk

P. 200-201
Photography, Styling SCHELTENS & ABBENES
www.scheltens-abbenes.com
Art Direction JOP VAN BENNEKOM
c/o ADM Art Director Management

P. 202-203
Photography, Styling SCHELTENS & ABBENES
www.scheltens-abbenes.com
Magazine Art Direction
JOP VAN BENNEKOM, GERT JONKERS
www.fantasticman.com

P. 204
Photography, Styling SCHELTENS & ABBENES
www.scheltens-abbenes.com
Art Direction FELIX BURRICHTER
www.pinupmagazine.org

P. 205
Photography, Styling SCHELTENS & ABBENES
www.scheltens-abbenes.com

P. 206-207
Photography FRANK STÖCKEL
www.frankstoeckel.de
c/o Lilamanagement
Art Direction SASCHA DETTWEILER
www.i-am-sad.com
Styling NINA LEMM
www.ninalemm.com c/o Liganord
Postproduction MAIK PRZYBYLSKI
www.albertbauer.com
Props AXIS MUNDI
www.axis-mundi.de

P. 208-209
Photography REINHARD HUNGER
www.reinhard-hunger.de
c/o Bransch
Styling CHRISTOPH HIMMEL
www.christophhimmel.de
c/o Liganord

P. 210-211
Photography JAN BURWICK
www.janburwick.de
c/o Wildfox Running
Styling CHRISTOPH HIMMEL
www.christophhimmel.de
c/o Liganord

P. 212-213
Photography REINHARD HUNGER
www.reinhard-hunger.de
c/o Bransch
Styling CHRISTOPH HIMMEL
www.christophhimmel.de
c/o Liganord

P. 214-215
Photography REINHARD HUNGER
www.reinhard-hunger.de
c/o Bransch
Styling, Food Styling VOLKER HOBL
www.volkerhobl.com

P. 216-217
Photography JUSTINE REYES
www.justinereyes.com

P. 218-219
Photography OLIVER SCHWARZWALD
www.oliverschwarzwald.de
Styling KIRSTEN SCHMIDT
www.kirsten-schmidt.eu
Magazine Fashion Direction
CHRISTINE ZERWES
www.stern.de

P. 220-221
Photography, Styling SARAH ILLENBERGER
www.sarahillenberger.com
Assistance SABRINA RYNAS
www.sabrina-rynas.com

P. 222
Photography ATTILA HARTWIG
www.attilahartwig.com
Styling SARAH ILLENBERGER
www.sarahillenberger.com

P. 223
Photography, Styling SARAH ILLENBERGER
www.sarahillenberger.com

P. 224-225
Photography DAN TOBIN SMITH
www.dantobinsmith.com
Styling, Set Design LEILA LATCHIN
www.leilalatchin.com

P. 226-227
Photography, Art Direction RYAN HOPKINSON
www.ryanhopkinson.co.uk
Styling, Art Direction ANDREW STELLITANO
www.astarism.co.uk
Matte Painting ADAM LEARY
www.adamleary.com
Postproduction THE FORGE
www.theforgeuk.com

P. 228-229
Photography MICHAEL BAUMGARTEN
www.michaelbaumgarten.com
Set Design ANNA BURNS
www.annaburns.net

P. 230
Photography STEVE GALLAGHER
www.stevegallagher.com

P. 231
Photography STEVE GALLAGHER
www.stevegallagher.com
Styling KATIE FORTIS
www.katiefortis.com

P. 232
Photography MAURIZIO DI IORIO
www.mauriziodiiorio.com
Styling MI DONG
www.cargocollective.com/midong

P. 233-247
Photography MAURIZIO DI IORIO
www.mauriziodiiorio.com

P. 248-249
Photography WYNE WEEN
www.wyneveen.com
Postproduction PATRICK DEBAS
www.dogpostproduction.com

P. 250-251
Photography AARON TILLEY
www.aarontilley.com
Set Design GEMMA TICKLE
www.gemmatickle.com

P. 252-253
Photography AARON TILLEY
www.aarontilley.com
Set Design, Styling KYLE BEAN
www.kylebean.co.uk
Foodstyling IAIN GRAHAM
www.iaingrahamchef.com

P. 254-255
Photography, Styling, Art Direction
RAW COLOR
www.rawcolor.nl
Art Direction NOWNESS
www.nowness.com

P. 256-257
Photography GUSTAV ALMESTAL
c/o LundLund www.almestal.com
Food Styling NIKLAS HANSEN
www.niklashansen.se

P. 258-259
Photography SAM HOFMAN
www.samhofman.co.uk
Styling ANDREW STELLITANO
www.astarism.co.uk

P. 260-261
Photography BELA BORSODI
www.belaborsodi.com
Prop Styling JOJO LI
www.studiojojoli.com
Food Styling VICTORIA GRANOF
www.victoriagranof.com

P. 262-263
Photography BELA BORSODI
www.belaborsodi.com
PropStyling JOJO LI
www.studiojojoli.com
Fashion Styling VANESSA GIUDICI
c/o Quadriga

P. 264-265
Photography BELA BORSODI
www.belaborsodi.com

P. 266-267
Photography BLOMMERS SCHUMM
www.blommers-schumm.com

P. 268
Photography, Concept, Styling, Set Design,
Postproduction PETER LANGER
www.peter-langer.com
Magazine Art Direction JASMIN MÜLLER-STOY
www.müllerundstoy.de
Magazine Creative Direction MIRKO BORSCHE
www.mirkoborsche.com
Magazine Fashion Direction TILLMANN PRÜFER
www.zeit.de
Magazine Picture Editing ANDREAS WELLNITZ,
MILENA CARSTENS, MICHAEL BIEDOWICZ
www.zeit.de

P. 269
Photography, Concept, Set Design,
Postproduction PETER LANGER
www.peter-langer.com
Magazine Art and Creative Direction
ERIC PILLAULT
www.lemonde.fr
Magazine Style Direction LILI BARBERY-
COULON
www.lemonde.fr
Magazine Fashion Direction
ALEKSANDRA WORONIECKA
www.lemonde.fr
Magazine Photo Editing LUCY CONTICELLO
www.lemonde.fr
Magazine Art Direction Assistance
JEAN-BAPTISTE TALBOURDET-NAPOLEONE
www.jbtalbourdet.fr

P. 270-271
Photography PETER LANGER
www.peter-langer.com
Magazine Art Direction ANTON IOUKHNOVETS
www.achtung-mode.com
Magazine Creative and Fashion Direction
MARKUS EBNER
www.achtung-mode.com
Styling WINNIE PLACZKO
www.winnieplaczko.com
Photo Assistant SHINJI MINEGISHI
www.shinjiminegishi.com

P. 272-274
Photography, Concept, Styling, Set Design,
Postproduction PETER LANGER
www.peter-langer.com
Magazine Art Direction JASMIN MÜLLER-STOY
www.müllerundstoy.de
Magazine Creative Direction MIRKO BORSCHE
www.mirkoborsche.com
Magazine Fashion Direction TILLMANN PRÜFER
Magazine Picture Editing ANDREAS WELLNITZ,
MILENA CARSTENS, MICHAEL BIEDOWICZ
www.zeit.de

P. 275
Photography PETER LANGER
www.peter-langer.com
Magazine Art Direction PETER BREUL
www.faz.net
Fashion Direction ALFONS KAISER
www.faz.net
Creative Editing, Styling WINNIE PLACZKO
www.winnieplaczko.com

P. 276-279
Photography, Concept, Styling, Set Design,
Postproduction PETER LANGER
www.peter-langer.com
Magazine Art Direction JASMIN MÜLLER-STOY
www.müllerundstoy.de
Magazine Creative Direction MIRKO BORSCHE
www.mirkoborsche.com
Magazine Fashion Direction TILLMANN PRÜFER
Magazine Picture Editing ANDREAS WELLNITZ,
MILENA CARSTENS, MICHAEL BIEDOWICZ
www.zeit.de

P. 280
Photography, Concept, Styling, Set Design,
Postproduction PETER LANGER
www.peter-langer.com
Magazine Art Direction KATJA KOLLMANN
Magazine Creative Direction MIRKO BORSCHE
www.mirkoborsche.com
Magazine Fashion Direction TILLMANN PRÜFER
Magazine Picture Editing ANDREAS WELLNITZ,
MILENA CARSTENS, MICHAEL BIEDOWICZ
www.zeit.de
Photo Assistant SHINJI MINEGISHI
www.shinjiminegishi.com

P. 281
Photography, Concept, Styling, Set Design,
Postproduction PETER LANGER
www.peter-langer.com
Magazine Art Direction KATJA KOLLMANN
Magazine Creative Direction MIRKO BORSCHE
www.mirkoborsche.com
Magazine Fashion Direction TILLMANN PRÜFER
Magazine Picture Editing ANDREAS WELLNITZ,
MILENA CARSTENS, MICHAEL BIEDOWICZ
www.zeit.de
Styling ANETT STEINBRECHER
Photo Assistant SHINJI MINEGISHI
www.shinjiminegishi.com

P. 282-283
Photography, Concept MIRKA LAURA SEVERA
www.severafrahm.com
ArtDirection ERIC PILLAULT
www.lemonde.fr
Styling LILLY MARTHE EBENER
www.lillymarthe-ebener.com
Postproduction MICHAEL FRAHM
www.severafrahm.com

THE STILL LIFE

IN PRODUCT PRESENTATION AND EDITORIAL DESIGN

This book was conceived, edited, and designed by Gestalten.

Edited by Anna Sinofzik and Robert Klanten

Content page snippets written by Anna Sinofzik and Noelia Hobeika

Text written by Anna Sinofzik

Text edited by Noelia Hobeika

Front cover photography by Qiu Yang

Back cover photography by
Qiu Yang (top left)
Metz + Racine (top right)
Maurizio Di Iorio (bottom right)

Layout and design by Anna Sinofzik

Typeface: Archive Mono by Colophon Foundry, Nobel Regular by Font Bureau

Proofreading by Felix Lennert

Printed by Eberl Print GmbH
Made in Germany

Published by Gestalten, Berlin 2015
ISBN 978-3-89955-581-3

For more information, please visit www.gestalten.com.

Bibliographic information published by the Deutsche Nationalbibliothek:
The Deutsche Nationalbibliothek lists this publication in the Deutsche Nationalbibliografie;
detailed bibliographic data are available online at http://dnb.d-nb.de.

None of the content in this book was published in exchange for payment by commercial parties or
designers; Gestalten selected all included work based solely on its artistic merit.

This book was printed on paper certified according to the standard of FSC®.